THE POWER OF CREATIVITY

AN UNCOMMON GUIDE TO MASTERING YOUR
INNER GENIUS AND FINDING NEW IDEAS
THAT MATTER (BOOK 2)

BRYAN COLLINS

BECOME A WRITER TODAY

For A.

FOREWORD

Do you want proven and free advice that will help you become more creative and find better ideas?

If you sign up at becomeawritertoday.com/pocbonus, I'll send you a free video lesson based on this book. You'll also get exclusive extracts from my next book about creativity.

WAIT!

DID YOU CLAIM YOUR FREE BONUS?

VISIT

BECOMEAWRITERTODAY/POCBONUS.COM

1

THE RIVER

"CREATIVITY IS like carrying a bucket to the river."

It's an old saying about creativity from the Far East. The unprepared man or woman who goes down to the riverbank without a bucket finds it harder to draw from the well-spring of ideas because he or she can only cup so much water in their hands before it flows through their fingers.

The prepared person who brings a bucket to the river quenches their thirst, fills their bucket and brings a generous helping back to their friends, family or peers.

In the West, people concerned about creativity care less about buckets and more about those moments of inspiration when an idea arrives as if from above.

It's no wonder the creative process and figuring out where great ideas come from feels so mystifying.

I've felt fascinated and mystified by the creative process for years. I wanted to discover more about how past creative masters like Leonardo da Vinci, Henri Matisse, and Albert Einstein and modern day creative masters like Steve Jobs, Elizabeth Gilbert, and John Cleese found their big ideas.

I set out to discover their insights into fresh thinking and whether they knew a secret hidden from the rest of us.

I found that creative masters fill their buckets with hundreds of little ideas – the ones that seem crazy, outlandish or foolish – and then, they distil what they find into a single powerful, big idea.

You too can find little ideas (and later distil them into big ones that matter) if you come down to the river prepared. In the pages to come, I will show you how.

Is This Book for You?

This book is the *second in a three-part series* about creativity, which I wrote for new writers, musicians, filmmakers, and artists.

The first book in this series – *The Power of Creativity: Learning How to Build Lasting Habits, Face Your Fears and Change Your Life* – was for writers, artists and musicians who felt adrift.

This second book is for anyone who has ever thought: 'how can I make something genuinely original?' or 'how can I get more ideas?' or 'what's the best way to focus on my ideas and just let them flow?'

Now, you don't need to be a genius or possess some mystical talent to become more creative at your chosen craft. Instead, you just need to know where to look for ideas; and if you're a writer, musician or artist wondering where to look, this book will help you.

Over the proceeding chapters, you'll gain chosen techniques for generating ideas. You'll also discover how to adopt the mindset of creative masters like Albert Einstein, Henri Matisse and Steve Jobs to get better at your craft and to unlock fresh thinking.

In each chapter, I'll draw on scientific and academic studies alongside more contemporary and even personal stories about creativity so you can unlock fresh thinking.

This book is as much practical as it is informative. At the end of each chapter, I'll also give you Creative Takeaways you can use to improve the quality and quantity of your little (and big) ideas.

What You're About to Discover About Fresh Thinking and Finding Great Ideas

So where can you find great ideas?

Well, they're everywhere... if you know where to look.

And look we shall.

In this book, I'll cover how to capture free-flowing thoughts, organise your thinking and come up with lots of little ideas faster using proven creative techniques from academia and the toolboxes of accomplished writers and artists.

The good news is you don't need to be an expert in your chosen field or craft to look for or even to come up with little or big ideas; in fact being an outsider gives you a unique perspective.

There's more...

When you're an outsider, you're more open to experimenting with form and substance, and that open-mindedness will help you inject a little bit of Henri Matisse or Albert Einstein's thinking into your work.

Then, things are going to get ambiguous.

You see here's the open secret about creativity:

There are no original ideas; there are only old ideas retold and combined in different ways.

Now I don't want you to be accused of being a thief, so I'll show you how to use other people's ideas without compromising your sense of ethics (or getting sued) as well as how to build on the work of your creative heroes.

And then, are you open to asking and answering a few difficult questions?

I ask because cultivating an intense sense of curiosity is an essential part of the creative process and you can do it using a simple technique from the business world.

There's a mindset successful creative people adopt too. Call it flow, call it a fugue, call it total immersion: I'll show you how creative masters turn on and off this mindset at will and how you can do the same.

In the end, unlocking fresh thinking means being open to the world around you. Later when the moment comes, you'll act on your ideas because you know there's lots to be done.

Now, the river lies just ahead: are you ready to dive in?

2

GO PROSPECTING FOR IDEAS

"To have a great idea, have a lot of them."
– Thomas Edison

I LOOK for ideas at home and in work. I capture them on the bus, on the train and when I wake at three am.

I don't write ideas down while driving the car because that's bad karma.

I write in the morning, at night, and sometimes in the afternoons – but I hate writing in the afternoon.

I capture ideas with my phone, on notepads and Moleskines (I once even wrote about Moleskines) and on the back of Post-Its.

I write ideas down on scraps of paper (God I love a great piece of blank paper), on the back of receipts, bills, bank statements and even on beer mats.

I record ideas while watching films and TV shows and cooking dinner. I write online, and I write in the woods. I write ideas down while connected and disconnected, plugged in, unplugged, wired and stone-cold sober.

Hey, Hemingway! It's always easier stone-cold sober.

I capture ideas on laptops and computers old and new. I write on Macs and PCs; I write with broken pens and unsharpened pencils.

I write ideas into the notes app on my phone, in WordPress, on Medium, Twitter, Facebook, LinkedIn and in every other box that fills my screen.

I write with broken things about broken things and for broken people. I write for myself.

I write down ideas until my head aches, and my heart spins.

So, I take a break...

Where was I?

I'm on the toilet with one leg hunched over the other, a pen in my hand and a big idea to chase down.

Come catch me, Bryan...

I'm trying, baby, slow down!

I write for food. I write for money. I write to pass the time. I write when I'm bored, lonely, angry or tired. Some days, I can't think of anything at all.

And that's always worse.

I consider new ideas in my head, and people turn and ask me, "What are you thinking about?"

"Don't disturb me, I've got an idea man, can't you see?"

"You're so crazy," they say.

But I don't care. I just write on and on.

It never stops.

Where and When Do You Write Ideas Down?

I'm telling you all of this because I want you to become fastidious about recording whatever pops into your mind, whether it's in a notebook, an app, or on a piece of blank paper.

Many artists keep a notebook beside their bed in case they dream of an idea during their sleep, wake up and want to capture it on paper before they forget.

You don't need a pretty or an expensive notebook and don't worry about recording the wrong things. Instead, write down five to ten ideas each morning or if you're uncomfortable writing, use a dictaphone or the recorder on your phone to capture melodies and fragments that pop into your mind.

Your goal is simply to practice coming up with ideas more frequently. Doing this trains your monkey mind to focus on the possibilities around you.

If you write ideas down every day, you'll increase the chances of having at least one or two actionable creative ideas by the end of the week, whereas the procrastinating artists who don't bother will reach the end of the week and find their bucket is empty.

But what if nothing useful or imaginative ever pops into your head? What if your imagination is barren and you can't fill your notebook or your recorder with ideas no matter how hard you try?

With some tenacity, you can drill down into your subconsciousness. Then, you can use three different powerful approaches for sifting through what you find and extracting a big or golden idea.

Approach 1: The Six Thinking Hats

In 1985, the academic Edward de Bono (born 1933) proposed the concept of *Six Thinking Hats* as a scientific way of coming up with more ideas that matter, faster. His *Six Thinking Hats* premise is easy to apply. Just consider your big idea while wearing six different metaphorical hats: a *Blue Hat*, *White Hat*, *Red Hat*, *Black Hat*, *Yellow Hat* and a *Green Hat*.

When you're tackling a new creative project, put on your *Blue Hat* to gain an overview of your big idea. Describe the process surrounding your idea. Consider what you want to explore, the problems you're having and your goal for the big idea in question.

Wearing my *Blue Hat* to describe this book, I can say it provides proven strategies for writers, musicians, artists and anyone who wants to overcome common creative challenges.

Next, don your imaginary *White Hat* and explain the facts about your big idea. Ask yourself what do you know about your big idea and what facts do you possess?

I wore my *White Hat* when I wanted to write an initial outline of this book and evaluate what I knew about creativity and what I needed to learn or read up on.

Your metaphorical *Red Hat* is for articulating emotions. Ask yourself what does your instinct or gut tell you about your big idea?

While tackling this project, my *Red Hat* thinking told me many people don't feel like they are creative. My gut told me they don't believe it's possible to become more creative.

Wear your *Black Hat* and view your big idea logically. Ask how can you approach your big idea in a sensible way? Your *Black Hat* thinking will help you become more critical of your big idea before you start working on it.

I wore my *Black Hat* and figured out that distilling my knowledge of creativity into applicable laws or strategies would make this book easier for people to read. I also found this approach would help me simplify the process of writing this book.

Wear your *Yellow Hat* to explore the benefits of your big idea. Ask yourself what are the benefits of your big idea and how will tackling it help you or your audience? Be optimistic and hopeful about how things will turn out.

In my case, I wore my *Yellow Hat* and figured out I could discover more about creativity if I wrote a book about it. My *Yellow Hat* thinking also told me I could help readers overcome common creative challenges.

Finally, wear your *Green Hat* for being more creative about your big idea. That means asking questions like: how can I approach my big idea using fresh thinking? What new ideas do I have?

In my case, I read various books about creativity, and I came up with strategies that struck me as original but also as a summation of what I'd learnt during the research process.

Now that you know how to use DeBono's *Six Thinking Hats*, it's time to put this strategy into practice using free writing.

The 50 Laws of Creativity (an early idea for this book)

Approach 2: Free Writing

Free writing is the rapid, non-judgmental capturing of ideas on paper (or in your word processor) as they rise to the top of your mind. It's a technique artists can use to generate ideas that matter and overcome feeling blocked or uninspired.

Mark Levy, author of *Accidental Genius: Using Writing to Generate Your Best Ideas, Insight, and Content* defines free writing as:

> "A fast method of thinking onto paper that enables you to reach a level of thinking that's often difficult to attain during the course of a normal business day."

I've used free writing in one form or another for years. The purpose of it is to get whatever is simmering in the back of your mind out of your head and onto a piece of paper. It doesn't matter if you what you write is plain daft or silly. The point is only to capture whatever your subconsciousness has been wrestling.

Think of free writing as exploratory drilling for oil – only it's better for the environment. It doesn't matter if you're not an accomplished writer because nobody is supposed to see the fruits of your free writing sessions.

Instead, they serve as a way of thinking out-loud on the page. When you finish free writing, you can go back and re-read what you wrote to see if there's anything you can extract. It's easy to sift through your subconscious for golden ideas through free writing.

WRITE FAST

Don't give your brain a moment to pause or evaluate your thoughts. It doesn't matter if you make typos or spelling mistakes while free writing - just keep getting the words out of your head and onto the blank page before the critical part of your brain has time to catch up.

Work Against a Limit:

I love limits because they give an artist confines within which to work. You can use a word count (the higher, the better), a deadline, or a timer.

I set a timer on my computer for 25 minutes, disconnect from the Internet, and free write as fast as I can without interruption. When the timer sounds, I take a break and evaluate my ideas.

Write What You See or Hear

Free writing isn't the time for editing, so jot down random ideas, swear words, and off-topic points. If you get interrupted while free writing, just write down that you were interrupted.

If you hear a dog barking on the street, and you remember that you need to feed your dog, write that down too. And if you think of an idea that has nothing to do with your creative challenge, follow your train of thought. These tangents are often the key to innovative work.

Express the Same Idea Multiple Ways

Expressing your idea multiple times helps you clarify it – and it's more productive than sitting around waiting for inspiration. Go back to your last idea and write it in a different way or from a different angle. If you're unsure of how to do this, ask yourself one of De Bono's questions on the page and free write your answer.

Write the Way You Think

When you free write, keep it conversational and use everyday language. You're not here to impress anyone and nobody is going to read what you're writing. So, jump around from one topic to the next, swear, and rage against your idea. Get the raw yolk of your big idea onto the page.

But I Don't Like Writing!

If the prospect of sitting down in front of the blank page induces nausea and you still need a way of drilling down for more ideas, fear not: there's another powerful creative strategy you can use.

Approach 3: Mind Mapping

Mind mapping is a proven and practical, creative technique for organising your ideas, research and finding more ideas that matter. Drawing a mind map, or mind mapping, is one of the best ways to establish links between your ideas and then see these connections in one place before you write.

Mind maps will also help you connect unrelated ideas, outline your work, and save time creating. What's more, mind maps serve as useful memory aids, and they're ideal for visual thinkers.

As Leonardo da Vinci said, "Everything is connected to everything else."

Modern science supports mind mapping as well.

Researchers at the University of Nottingham in the UK found drawings or visual representations (like mind maps) help people organise, break down, and remember complex topics.

When to Use Mind Maps

Mind maps are ideal for almost any creative work. The only caveat of this technique is that each mind map should focus on a specific idea.

You can use mind mapping to see the overall structure of a book or a film, think through an idea before setting to work on it, review what you learnt and even to organise areas of your creative life.

Creating Your Mind Map

Think of your mind map like a tree. The central idea is the root, and the related ideas serve as branches.

To create your first mind map, start simple.

Get an A4 white piece of paper and red, blue, and black pens. Turn the paper on its side and write your idea or topic in the centre of the page.

From there, draw the connecting ideas.

Using your coloured pens, write connecting ideas along the branches, shooting out from the central idea. These branches or lines should be thicker at the root and grow thinner as they move out from the central idea.

Map out all that comes to mind and work on your mind map for 10 or 15 minutes, without interruption.

Use Colours and Images

Red, blue, black, green markers will help you create a more visual and memorable mind-map. You should see the central idea, the overall structure, and how everything is connected at a glance.

You don't have to be great at drawing, either. It's enough to sketch simple images, representing key ideas on your mind map.

Don't fear making mistakes or obsess about the structure of your mind map. Instead, simply reorder your branches or draw another mind map if you need.

If you're using a whiteboard or digital tool, you can rearrange your mind map as you go.

Simplify Your Mind Maps

Although some mind mapping experts use complex mind maps, I find these are time-consuming to create and use; particularly, if you're unsure about how to use them for your creative work.

Experimenting with your mind maps is a good practice. You could try different pictures and colours, play with the shape and the way you branch and order your ideas.

Prune Your Mind Map

As you fill your mind map with your ideas, it will grow rapidly and in many directions. Like the artful gardener, it's your job to prune the tree and shape your mind map. When you've finished your first mind map, reorganise or remove what you don't need, so you can understand it later on.

Mind Mapping Your Way to an Idea That Works

Even if your mind map looks pretty, it's useless if you avoid doing anything with it.

Have a plan for turning your mind map into something you can write or create. Or if your mind map serves as a visual aid, print it out, and keep it with you for a while. I also save digital mind maps in Evernote.

Remember, your mind map is a creative strategy, but it's not the work.

How I Used a Mind Map to Write This Chapter

Before writing my first draft of this part of the chapter, I created a mind map. My central idea was to answer a question: "What is Mind Mapping?" After coming up with a central idea, I wrote down the main points of the chapter, based on what I'd read and researched.

Next, I expanded these main points and branched them out into sub-topics. I paid little attention to the order or structure of my ideas until I had finished.

After completing the first version of this mind map, I added colours and images to it. Next, I reorganised my mind map in a clockwise fashion. I put the introduction to the article at 1 o'clock, the "Why Mind Maps?" section at 3 o'clock, and so on.

Then, I pruned or removed what I didn't need. Creating the map took about 20 minutes. Finally, I dictated this chapter by looking at my sheet and speaking into a microphone about the topics I'd mapped.

You don't have to create a mind map, like this.

Some mind mapping aficionados put their central idea to the far left of the screen or page. Then, they branch out their ideas in a horizontal or a linear fashion, much like a Fishbone or cause and effect diagram.

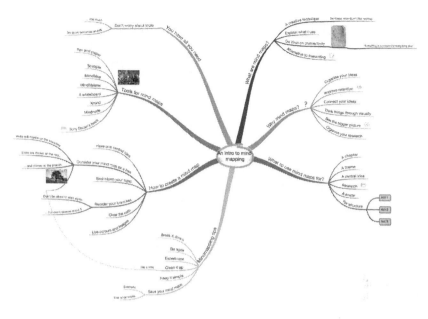

The mind map in question

What to Use for Creating Your Mind Maps

Yes, there are a number of digital tools and apps that can help you create a great looking mind map (see the end of this book), but if you're new to mind mapping, analogue tools work just fine.

Limits encourage you to become more resourceful, and in this case, focus on your single idea. Pen, paper, and multi-coloured pens are perfect mind mapping tools because they are affordable, available, and it's difficult to tinker with them.

I also like using a whiteboard for mind mapping, because I can use an eraser to redraw and reconstruct parts of the mind map as I go. Again, I find it impossible to tinker with the settings of a whiteboard.

If you use pen and paper or a whiteboard for mind mapping, take a picture of your mind map with your phone and save it to your computer.

I save these pictures in Evernote, alongside the rest of my research for books, blog posts, or articles. I like advanced digital features as much as the next person, but the mind mapping tool you use is always less important than the process.

If you're mind mapping for the first time, I suggest going low-tech. Multi-coloured pens and a large sheet of paper work fine.

All It Takes

Filling your bucket with great ideas is hard work, but you can extract more big or golden ideas from your subconscious and the world around you with the right strategy.

DeBono's *Six Thinking Hats* will help you ask better questions about whatever you're working on; free writing will help you explore ideas deep in your subconscious and mind mapping will help organise your ideas before you get started.

Once you practice prospecting for ideas and drawing connections between what you find, you'll solve the problem of a barren imagination. You'll have tapped into your inner genius.

All it takes is practice.

Creative Takeaways

- Get a timer, a pen and some paper. Set the timer for 30 minutes and free write or mind map about a creative problem you're facing. Don't stop to edit yourself or read your work until the buzzer sounds.
- During your free writing or mind mapping session, wear each one of De Bono's *Six Thinking Hats* to increase the quantity and improve the quality of your ideas.

3

EXPERIMENT WITH FORM AND SUBSTANCE

"An artist must never be a prisoner. Prisoner? An artist should never be a prisoner of himself, prisoner of style, prisoner of reputation, prisoner of success."

– Henri Matisse

IN 1887, Henri Matisse (1869-1954) began to study law and worked as a court administrator in Le Cateau-Cambrésis in Paris, but the trajectory of his life changed after a bout of appendicitis two years later. While recovering, he had little to do. So, his mother bought Henri a box of paints.

"From the moment I held the box of colours in my hands, I knew this was my life. I threw myself into it like a beast that plunges towards the thing it loves," he said.

Matisse abandoned law to study art and work under artists like the painter John Peter Russell. He created still life and landscape paintings before moving to more impressionistic works.

He first made his name as an expressionist painter in the vein of

Paul Cézanne and Marcel Duchamp. Critics regarded Matisse as an extremist and a wild beat or a Fauve. Later, he became famous for paintings like *Music* and *The Dance,* and for his sculptures. Throughout his career, his works were compared endlessly against those by his younger rival Pablo Picasso.

The American art collector and critic Leo Stein said about Matisse, "All his pictures were to give him a lot of trouble... He worked endlessly on his pictures until they were finished."

Matisse's troubles started each morning when he rose early to paint. He worked through the morning and again after lunch. In the evening, he enjoyed violin practice, a simple supper and an early bedtime. Throughout his career, he worked mostly alone, albeit with the help of assistants or models.

Matisse expressed and thought through his creative visions using a paintbrush, and he spent hours reworking his masterworks.

In 1908, he said he wanted to create art "for every mental worker, for the businessman as well as the man of letters, for example, a soothing, calming influence on the mind, something like a good armchair which provides relaxation from physical fatigue."

As Matisse grew older and more successful, his critics regarded him as a creative master known for expressive colours and sensual works. He also explored other forms like drawings and sculptures and was able to bring insight from one form to the next.

"I sculpted as a painter," said Matisse, "I did not sculpt like a sculptor."

Then, in 1941, Matisse was diagnosed with abdominal cancer.

The 74-year-old artist underwent a serious operation in Lyon, which he didn't expect to survive. The surgery left Matisse chair and bed-bound, and he was unable to move about easily to paint or sculpt.

After this operation, Matisse faced regular and complicated procedures to maintain his digestive system, and he recognised he was approaching the end of his life.

Many other creative people would have put their tools down and considered their most important work complete. Instead, Matisse regarded his declining health as a creative challenge to overcome and believed he was living a "second life."

In an echo of what had happened when his mother bought a twenty-year-old Henri a box of paints, an elderly Matisse embraced a bolder artistic form, that of the scissors and coloured paper.

With the help of his assistant, he created a series of large colourful collages from cut paper and covered the walls of his bedroom with them. These cut-outs varied in colour and size, and some became room-sized works and murals.

Matisse published the first of these cut-outs as a series of illustrations in the book *Jazz* in 1947, and by 1948 he stopped painting altogether to focus on this form.

"I have attained a form filtered to its essentials," an elderly Matisse said about this new medium, which he used to express his joy of life.

His cut-outs portrayed lively compositions of dancers, musicians, swimmers, the circus, clowns, funerals and animals while others evoked images of death and war. They also represent a stunning and original chapter in the artist's long creative career, and they were relished by the critics of the day.

In 1951, an American critic said about Matisse's final works: "Never before has Matisse seemed to me so young."

Three years later Matisse died of a heart attack.

His life and art demonstrate how changing the form and substance of your creative works can enable better, bolder ideas and more inspired thinking.

Instead, of holding too tightly to a way of working that you trust, consider how else you can express yourself and what you could do if your tools, your resources and even your health were stripped away.

Why Should You Experiment With Form and Substance?

Because Matisse told you so!

Firstly, if you feel blocked or stuck, experimenting with form is a relieving remedy.

The constrictions of your chosen medium may not be ideal for expressing your idea, and a little experiment (like a cardboard cut-out) could help you find a better means of expression.

Ideas are everywhere; they are free flowing and formless. It's your job to form them into something tangible that engages your audience.

The form surrounding your big ideas will shift over the lifetime of your project, so, please don't solidify it prematurely because you want the work to be done.

Remember too it's your responsibility to get your ideas in front of as many people as possible. Presenting your ideas in different forms will help your audience engage in a way that suits them.

This isn't derivative. It isn't lazy. And it's not uninspired.

What if, for example, a would-be reader of your book is blind or prefers to listen to audio? Will you create an audio book so they can engage with your ideas?

It's also less exhausting to transform one good idea that works into a different form than it is to come up with a second idea. And a third. And a fourth.

You're doing yourself (and your would-be audience) a great disservice by not considering how you might transform your idea into different forms to engage different people.

Finally, have you ever had the experience of studying under one teacher for months only to find it all but impossible to learn what they were trying to teach?

Then, later, another teacher addresses the same topic, and everything falls into place? In many cases, it's not that the second teacher was more accomplished than the first. Instead, listening to an idea multiple times, told in different ways helps it sink in.

You can help your ideas sink in through creative experimentation.

How to Experiment With Form and Substance

Matisse experimented with the canvas, clay and paper to express his ideas. Whether you're a writer, artist or musician, you have even more opportunities than Matisse to experiment with form and substance.

Austin Kleon is an American writer, artist and poet who uses digital and analogue tools to experiment with his form and substance.

Kleon composes poetry and creates art, but in an unusual way. He cuts out newspaper clippings, blackens the text with a felt-tip marker, leaving behind only certain words and phrases that form a poem.

He documents the process for creating his poems alongside the final result in his books, on his website and Instagram. In his book *Steal Like an Artist*, Kleon writes about his creative experiments:

> "The process engaged most of my senses: the feel of newsprint in my hands, the sight of words disappearing under my lines, the faint squeak of the marker tip, the smell of the marker fumes--there was a kind of magic happening. When I was making the poems, it didn't feel like work. It felt like play."

Creative experimentation for writers was difficult in Matisse's time due to the costs of printing but today digital tools enable any writer to experiment with the length and form of their works.

Hugh Howey is an American science-fiction writer. In 2011, he began self-publishing a series of short stories about a dystopian, post-nuclear holocaust world.

His self-published short stories were a hit on Amazon, so Howey combined them into a novella and later a book called *Wool* before publishing the series *Silo*. He then released audiobooks of his popular series.

Howey understands that audiobooks enable new readers to find his book and that audio lends lend a sense of life and urgency to his work.

In 2012, he signed a traditional book publishing deal and 20th Century Fox/Lionsgate bought the film rights to his book.

Howey cares less about the old rules of publishing books; his mission is to get his stories out in front of as many people as possible. On his blog, he writes:

> "You are writing for the reader, who is your ultimate gatekeeper. Get your work in front of them, even if it's one at a time, one reader a month or year."

But what if you compose music?

Take heart from how Glen Hansard, Markéta Irglová and John Carney transformed their music and stories.

Irishman Glen Hansard is the frontman of *the Frames* and one-half of folk rock duo, *The Swell Season with* Markéta Irglová, while John Carney is an Irish film and TV writer.

In 2007, Carney wrote a movie script about a struggling thirty-something busker who falls in love with a folk singer and single mother from the Czech Republic. He invited his friend Glen (they played together in *The Frames* years ago) and Irglová to star in the film, for which they also wrote the soundtrack.

The events on-screen mirrored events off-screen in that Hansard and Irglová were, for a time, a real-life couple and they appeared to portray characters similar to themselves.

The film became a commercial success, and Hansard and Irglová won an Oscar for writing the song *Falling Slowly*.

Although *Once* is a worldwide hit today, it's worth remembering this film started as a small indie project shot over three weeks with a modest budget of just over EUR112,000.

What's even more significant is that Hansard and Irglová first released the music of *Once* as a *Swell Season* record and only sold 300 copies.

After they had the attention of an audience, they re-released the album with a different cover and marketed it as a soundtrack for *Once*, and it went gold.

Hansard told Pitchfork:

> "But I couldn't believe that this record I put out with Mar, that I was really proud of, only sold 300. Then six months or a year later it gets re-released as the *Once* record. Four days ago I just heard that it went gold over here. That's half a million fucking records! That's insane! That is fucking insane. And all we did was change the cover [laughs]."

The team behind *Once*, like many creative masters, know the value of repurposing great ideas.

The Irish playwright Enda Walsh transformed *Once* into a musical for Broadway, which went on to win eight Tony awards. Finally, the creative team behind *Once* took the musical to Ireland, England, Australia and Korea.

Contemporary Experimentation: The Sawdust Approach

Gary Vaynerchuk (born 1975) is an entrepreneur, investor, public speaker and social media expert. An energetic man from Belarus in the former USSR, he lives in Queens, New York with his family.

Vaynerchuk has built up multiple businesses including his family's wine business and more recently the digital marketing agency Vaynermedia.

He's also the author of four books and is a master of creating content to promote his businesses and his ideas in the form of articles, video clips, infographics, social media updates, podcast and YouTube episodes.

Although Gary has an entire team behind him today, for years he created his content almost entirely by himself. The volume and intensity of Gary's work would exhaust a reasonable man or woman.

So how did Gary do it? Is he superhuman?

Gary says, "It was just me doing my thing."

He excels at taking a single great idea and transforming it repeatedly for different platforms. In an opening to one recent blog post, Gary writes,

> "I'm about to get real meta on you: the article you're about to read was made from a video, that was made from the making of an article, that was originally based off a video."

When Gary is launching a book, he creates content around the book that informs his YouTube show, podcast, blog posts and social media updates. The ideas don't vary much from one medium to the next. Instead, Gary tailors his language and how he presents his ideas for each platform and audience.

Gary's experimentation with form and substance enables him to reach different audiences in different places without running out of resources, energy or time. He likens this approach to figuring out his sawdust, saying:

> "It's the byproducts of your output whether you're a podcaster or a writer or entrepreneur. It's someone who took the sawdust after cutting a bunch of 2x4s, repackaging it and then selling it."

Gary recommends entrepreneurs, marketers, writers, artists and anyone with an idea to share or repurpose (or change the form of) their work as much as possible because this is the best way to reach a wider audience.

> "Create content around the topics in your book, and make sure that content brings value to the consumers you most want to target. You'll create buzz around your brand and book, and people will see that you know what you're talking about. Then they'll only want to buy your book more, right?"

I worked as a content marketer for a software company, and it was my job to write articles and blog posts and transform these into ebooks, infographics, social media posts and more.

At first, I was uncomfortable with this way of working. It felt lazy and uninspired (sorry Gary). I liked the idea of sitting down to a blank canvas or a blank screen every time and coming up with something new, something better.

I quickly discovered when you're up against a deadline, and you've got a tight budget, reinventing the wheel every time isn't possible.

Even if you have lots of resources, you're doing your audience a disservice if you haven't tried to get your ideas in front of as many people as possible.

If someone reads a blog post, that doesn't mean they'll download an ebook, just as a podcast listener isn't always the same person as YouTube viewer (or a musical fan isn't necessarily a film buff).

So, with the help of a graphic designer, I turned chapters and key findings from an ebook into an eye-catching infographic and social media updates and in doing so we were able to reach more people.

Now, here's a secret about this book:

Some of the chapters you're reading started life as blog posts, which I later reworked, polished and turned into writing that's more appropriate for a book than a blog. Rewriting these posts as book chapters helped me think them through a little deeper and it's a fantastic way to squeeze more life from an idea.

Whether you're a writer, musician or artist, examine what you've already created. Then, consider who hasn't discovered your work and figure out if you can change the form of your ideas, if you can repackage your sawdust and serve a new audience. Because ideas that matter transcend traditional forms of expression.

Form and Music

Passing through the doors of the Hermitage museum, a bolt of pain shot across my temple, and my stomach lurched. I'd been up till three am the night before with four friends drinking Platinka vodka and eating black caviar in a traditional restaurant in St. Petersburg.

Having only four days to see Russia, we rose early after our boozy night out, walked down the bank of the Volga river and into Hermitage. But, I lacked the energy or willpower to spend the rest of the day browsing the sights in one of the world's largest and oldest museums.

I trundled from one room of this former Russian palace to the next sipping a bottle of sparkling water, until finally, I reached the Hercules Room. When I saw what was in there, I forgot about my hangover.

Henri Matisse's *Dance* and *La Musique* hung side-by-side on one of the red walls, apart from the rest of the masterpieces.

Dance is a canvas painting of five naked men and women who look like folk figures from a fairy tale. They're pulling each other and dancing around in a violent circle on top of a green hill holding hands.

In *La Musique*, two of the five folk figures are playing the violin and pipe while the others are sitting on the grass, their hands on their knees, their black eyes, ears, and mouths opening as the music plays.

In both paintings, the robust dark reds, greens and blues come alive, and when you look at these men and women long enough, they seem to shine, to move, to dance.

It's as if Matisse is still playing music for us some sixty years after his death using his paintbrush.

On my way out of the museum, I bought a print of *La Musique* and when I got home I framed it and hung it on the wall next to where I write.

When I'm stuck, feel uninspired, and my bucket runs empty, I look at Matisse's work to remind myself what's possible through experimenting with form and substance.

Creative Takeaways

- Pick one of your most recent creative projects. Extract an idea and experiment with it.
- Repackage your successful ideas into different forms and serve different audiences.

4

CHANGE YOUR PERSPECTIVE

"After all these years, I have come to realise that I must go through a period of agony and torture before I have a breakthrough."
– Hans Zimmer

"WHERE ARE YOU GOING NEXT?"

I was sick of this question.

I was nearly two months into a summer backpacking trip around Brazil, and I'd begun to loathe the backpackers around me. They kept asking me questions – not because they cared about my answer, but so they could prove their experience were more valid – and I was tired of it.

I guess I was jealous.

I was searching for an answer that didn't sound cliché, so when a crusty backpacker suggested the Pantanal I jumped at the chance of an experience far from the beaten track.

The world's largest swampland, the Pantanal is located mostly in Brazil, just below the Amazon jungle. To get there, I travelled on a bus for 12 hours in a cramped seat by a leaky toilet, and me with a wide grin that said, "This is roughing it."

Arriving at camp, I was struck by the novel soundtrack of the Pantanal: a cacophony of chattering monkeys and birds chirping in the trees and the rustle of bats flying overhead.

Our guide, Nikola, was a stocky man with bloodshot eyes and a series of scars around one of his forearms.

He flashed his torch onto the ground and said:

"Don't go the toilet cubicle without a torch."

I couldn't see much more than a metre in front of me, and when I looked down, I was shocked by the mass of ants swirling over my feet.

At breakfast the next morning, we swatted flies from our watermelons and pineapples, and then started what turned out to be a seven-hour trek through the forest and savannah land. Nikola dismissed our attempts at small talk with a grunt or a nod.

Still, his perception of the landscape was unlike ours. I'd see a mark in the sand or walk past a bush rustling and think nothing of it until Nikola explained the mark in the sand was a snake trail and that there was a monkey inside the bush.

Later, a group of lemurs charged across our path – their yellow and black tails bouncing in the air like a sea of frustrated hairballs.

That afternoon, we went horse riding.

I lagged behind the rest of the group. Every time I tried to direct the horse in one direction, it trotted in the other.

I was grateful when Nikola swapped his horse with mine. Five minutes later, the same protesting horse, reared in the air and flung our guide to the ground.

Nikola jumped up, grabbed the horse by the reins, smacked it in the face and stared into its eyes. The animal went quiet, and Nikola climbed back into the saddle. Then our horses rode us back to camp, breaking into a gallop as we drew near.

That night, a skinny man with a pockmarked face pulled an anaconda from the inside of a tree. He held it in the air and then, perhaps because I was standing closest, he thrust the wriggling snake into my hands.

He grinned at my shocked expression.

"Put it back in the tree," he said "Good luck."

I could feel the raw power of the animal pulsing through my arms.

After my friends had taken a photo, I dropped the snake onto the ground and walked off, very quickly.

Over a local sour drink, I asked our guide Nikola about the scars on his forearm.

He waved the aforementioned hand.

"Puma."

In broken English, Nikola confessed he dreamt of travelling on the Orient Express one day. But he explained he hadn't left the camp in over six months. It was his home and his work.

His dreams for his future were being shaped by his day-to-day experiences in the Pantanal just as mine were shaped by my mundane experiences at home in Ireland.

Early the next morning, we went fishing for piranhas. Nikola explained piranha also means 'slut' because "they will eat anything."

Much later, I read online that only certain breeds attack humans and even those breeds are only attracted to blood.

Then, a friend pointed out to what looked like an alligator at the edge of the lake.

"They are more afraid of us than you are of them."

Nikola proceeded to skin a piranha and toss the remains into a snapping alligator's mouth.

That night, we ate barbecued fish and boiled rice.

After dinner, Nikola asked us to shine our torches onto a lake at the back of the camp. Dozens of red eyes were gliding soundlessly through the water and away from the light. Looking at those alligators, my belly full of piranhas, it was hard not to feel pleased about this different view of the world.

While I took photos, Nikola stood to the side and looked at his watch. The absurdity of eating piranhas (they were bland and boney) and watching alligators was an alien experience from anything I'd done at home in Ireland, but Nikola had seen all this, many times.

The Unique Perspective of an Outsider

The German composer Hans Zimmer (born 1957) spent much of his spare time as a child and teenager composing music and playing with synthesisers.

As a young man, he played in clubs and bars with up and coming pop bands and also composed jingles for a BBC mini-series broadcast in the UK.

In the late 1980s, director Barry Levinson hired Zimmer to compose a soundtrack for his film *Rain Man*. Although this was Zimmer's big break, he was still an outsider. He felt afraid that he didn't know what he was doing and that his creative peers would expose him.

Instead, Zimmer was surprised to find Hollywood musicians were using technology that was years behind what he had used in Europe. In many cases, the directors only heard a score for the first time when the entire orchestra had assembled.

Zimmer saw this as an incredibly unproductive way to compose music, so he used his experiences as a European composer to play a score for Barry Levinson on a computer.

"Instead of making him imagine what the French horns would sound like, I'd bring them in on a computer," Zimmer told Gillian Segal in *Getting There*.

Rain Man won an Oscar for best picture, and Zimmer received a nomination for best soundtrack. Subsequently, he composed iconic soundtracks for films like *Driving Miss Daisy* and the *Pirates of the Caribbean* series. He also won an Oscar for composing the soundtrack for *The Lion King*.

Zimmer found creative success in a way his peers couldn't because he was an expert and because he possessed the unique perspective of an outsider, but even a master of Zimmer's talents would face many challenges.

In the late 2000s, Christopher Nolan hired Zimmer to compose the soundtrack for the *Dark Knight* series. The second film in this series is a particular dark thriller, and Zimmer (always in search of a novel idea) wanted to compose music "that people would truly hate."

During his search for this distinctive sound, Zimmer composed 90,000 bars of experimental music. One of his more absurd ideas involved striking razor blades against piano strings to get the haunting melody he was looking for.

Even then, Zimmer was unhappy with the results:

> "On the last day of recording with a one-hundred-person orchestra, I found myself lying on the couch in the back of the room experiencing terrible chest pains. I hadn't slept in weeks and was thinking, I'm going to die. But I didn't say anything. Chris Nolan, the director, who knows me very well, saw that I was in serious trouble. He walked over to the microphone and announced to the musicians, "I think we've recorded enough. You can all go home." I sat up and said, "No, no, no, no! We haven't!" Chris repeated, "I think we've recorded enough." And, of course, he was right.

The German philosopher Arthur Schopenhauer investigated the purpose of music extensively in his essays and writings. He argued great music helps the artist and listener understand the essence of our reality and the striving that underlies and unifies the universe.

In Zimmer's case, he was searching for a dark reality, which may go some way to explaining his creative struggles. Eventually, Zimmer found a more relevant sound by settling on a single note played on the cello by his colleague Martin Tillman. After listening to the final soundtrack, director Chris Nolan said exploring it was "a pretty unpleasant experience."

Zimmer was delighted; this was his intention and his iconic soundtrack was nominated for an Oscar. Today, Zimmer is an accomplished composer who Hollywood directors and producers seek out, but he still believes he must go through "a period of agony and torture" before achieving a breakthrough.

For him, the river is a dark place.

Despite his creative setbacks, Zimmer pushes himself to avoid fixed ways of thinking, and he advises new artists who want to do the same to try something new every day.

Karl Duncker would agree.

The Curious Case of Duncker's Candle

The German psychologist Karl Duncker (1903-1940) developed a problem-solving challenge known as Duncker's Candle, which was published posthumously in 1945.

He presented participants with a table propped against a wall, on top of which were a packet of matches, a box of thumbtacks and a candle. He then asked participants to attach the candle to the wall and prevent any wax from dripping from the candle onto the table below.

If you're thinking about a solution to this creative problem, you've got five minutes.

The first time I faced *Duncker's Candle* problem, I decided the answer lay in attaching the candle to the wall using the tacks.

Like many students' answers, my solution felt perfectly reasonable, and it was perfectly wrong. Pressing thumbtacks into a waxy candle is messy and inefficient. I also came across other answers where students decided to melt the candle and use the hot wax to attach it to the wall.

So what's wrong with all of these solutions?

Well, they're overly complicated, and they rely on a fixed view of the world.

Instead, all you have to do is pick up the box of thumbtacks and empty the thumbtacks onto the table. Now, use a single thumbtack to attach the box to the wall, and then put the candle into the box.

Simple, isn't it?

Here's the thing: *Duncker's Candle* Problem reveals many of us are attached to rigid definitions of what's possible and impossible.

We fail to see the box as a separate object that we can use to solve the problem. We're afraid of breaking the rules and doing things in abnormal or absurd ways. In the end, because of our fixed perspective, the quality of our ideas suffers.

The good news is you can find practical and novel ideas if you know where to start and if you're prepared to leave common sense behind (if only for a little while).

From the Absurd to the Relevant

How can you find an idea that's novel and useful, as Hans Zimmer did with the *Dark Knight* soundtrack?

Well, I'd like you to think of your creative project as a mountain. At the top of this mountain, you can mine bizarre, outlandish and absurd ideas and at the bottom of the mountain you can extract practical, relevant and logical ideas.

Now, you're not looking to set up camp at the top of this mountain because the conditions up there are too inhospitable for your ideas to thrive. There's also little point in settling at the bottom of this mountain because basecamp is a crowded place; we've all been there before.

Instead, there's a hidden place between the points of absurdity and relevancy that is rich in novel ideas and useful ideas. Think of it as like a secret forge where you can combine the novelty of the absurd with the applicability of the practical. Here, your inner genius can get to work and smelt the golden ideas you crave.

The question is: how can you get to this secret forge while expending a minimal amount of your limited creative resources?

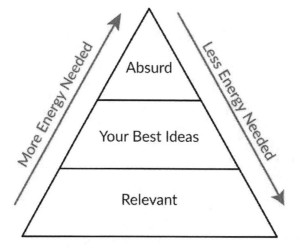

Create a Thought Experiment

If a teacher, friend, family member or colleague has ever said, "you live inside your head," you'll recognise this as a perplexing and sometimes embarrassing experience.

I know because this happens to me regularly, but the next time someone criticises you for this behaviour, tell them you're engaging in a thought experiment, that you're thinking your ideas through just like Albert Einstein (1879-1955).

They'll probably look at you like you're crazy, but here's the thing: your imagination will help you get to the top of the mountain to mine your absurd ideas.

Just like Albert Einstein.

He lived in his head for hours at a time, where he conducted thought experiments or *Gedankenexperimente*. During these exercises, he took an idea or a scenario and spun it around in his mind.

As a young schoolchild in Aarau in Switzerland, Einstein attempted to picture what it would be like to ride alongside a light beam. He said:

> "In Aarau I made my first rather childish experiments in thinking that had a direct bearing on the Special Theory. If a person could run after a light wave with the same speed as light, you would have a wave arrangement which could be completely independent of time. Of course, such a thing is impossible."

It's easy to imagine Einstein's teacher telling him to stop daydreaming and pay attention to the lesson in front of him.

Einstein later credited this thought experiment as the starting point for his *Theory of Relativity*. During his late twenties and early thirties, he used mathematical equations and the rigour of science to take his absurd idea and formulate an applicable theory.

Some of Einstein's other thought experiments involved lightning strikes, falling painters, moving trains and even imagining the velocity of electrons.

While Einstein gave time to daydreams and his imagination, he eventually uprooted ideas from the recesses of his mind, wrote them down, worked on them and published his findings.

In other words, he climbed down from his absurd daydreams about running after light or imagining the speed of an electron and turned his thoughts into practical scientific concepts.

The Practical and Absurd Creative Mind

The next time you're struggling with a creative project, try to come up with as many absurd ideas as possible. Like with the free writing exercise I described in an earlier chapter, push past your point of comfort and cognitive biases and have fun with your ideas, fantasies and daydreams. Strike razor blades against the piano string, if you will.

Now, let's say I want to come up with a creative way of promoting a new novel. Here are three absurd promotional ideas:

- Hire a plane to paint the book title in the sky over crowds at Wembley football stadium.
- Tattoo the title of the book to my face.
- Stand naked on O'Connell Street in Dublin City Centre while reading my book out loud and streaming said recording on Facebook.

Once you have these absurd ideas, work your way down to what's relevant – move from razor blades toward the cello playing a single note. The climb down is always easier. In the case of the above example, here's what I came up with:

- Give away 500 copies of the book to bloggers, would-be readers and reviewers and offer one of their readers a holiday.
- Mock up a photograph of me with this tattoo in Photoshop and use this for a Facebook advertising campaign.
- Record myself reading my book out loud at locations featured in the book (standing the Giant's Causeway, on a boat to the Aran Islands etc.) around Ireland and upload these recordings to YouTube.

James Altucher is a successful self-published author who is adept at book promotions and someone who moves from the absurd to the relevant with ease.

James didn't tattoo the title of his best-selling self-published book *Choose Yourself* to his face. Instead, he made a t-shirt with every word from his book printed on it and then proceeded to give away these t-shirts to would-be readers and reviewers.

Remember, it's okay to explore hunches, probe new avenues of thought and bring back anything unusual or odd that you find. Later on, sift through these discoveries and figure out what's usable and what to put aside. Your creative ideas are never wrong, not even the absurd ones.

Creative masters like Hans Zimmer and Albert Einstein change their perspectives as often as they can because even the novel and fresh become...

Old and Stale

On the last day of my trip to the Pantanal, Nikola woke us before dawn. The sun stepped lazily onto the horizon and light trickled down across the fields.

It was a beautiful Brazilian morning, but I was tired of the chirping birds and monkeys, the bats flying overhead at night, of being bitten by ants, slapping mosquitos from my arms and my tongue turning numb from the taste of repellant.

I'd had enough of the Pantanal, the early mornings, the uncomfortable heat and using a torch to go to the toilet. The camp felt old, fixed and confining.

We watched the sun light up the dirt track leading to the camp. A jeep was carrying a new group of backpackers towards us. My off-the-beaten track experience only felt unique compared to where I'd been before and where I was going next.

I thought of Rio de Janeiro and about football, sex and religion. Change was coming, and I relished it.

I didn't think much about the Pantanal again until months later back in Ireland. There, during grey days in the office park where I worked, I wondered if Nikola was still fantasising about the Orient Express while leading tourists around the savannahs and forests.

I fought with the photocopier and imagined what would happen if we were attacked by pumas at 3.37 pm on a random Tuesday. A colleague, seeing me lost in thought, asked what I was thinking about.

When I told her, she said, "That's absurd."

Creative Takeaways

- Set time aside to day-dream and for thought experiments.
- Write down 100 ideas. They should be as extreme and as absurd as possible. Now climb down from these ideas to what's relevant.

5

EMBRACE CONSTRAINTS OF TIME
AND MONEY

"Don't give me any money, don't give me any people, but give freedom, and I'll give you a movie that looks gigantic."
– Robert Rodriguez

AN ACCOMPLISHED TAILOR once told me he listens to what his customers want before showing them three suits.

"Why three suits?" I asked.

"I never give a customer too much choice," he said. "The customer will just find it harder to come to a decision."

This tailor understands that the human brain dislikes too many choices whereas constraints simplify decision-making.

So how does this apply to your creative work?

Well, have you ever heard someone say:

"If only I had more money, then I could do it."

Or:

"I don't have time to paint today."

Or:

"I don't have time to write today."

Many aspiring creative people come out with things like this when the time comes to write, paint, play or draw.

The harsh truth is these people are making excuses.

If you want to become more creative, you must recognise you don't need more resources, time or energy. These things are not your friends. They lead to bloat and excess.

Working on an idea is often more about problem solving than it is about having a bright white canvas before you and unlimited resources at your disposal.

Instead of being concerned about what you lack, you can use constraints of time, money and resources as a float to guide you down the river, as a means of becoming *more creative*, just like accomplished photographers, film-makers and musicians have done before you.

Turning What You Lack into a Creative Asset

One of ten children, Texas-born Robert Rodriguez (born 1968) wanted to become a filmmaker just like John Carpenter. His earliest memories are of going to an old movie theatre in San Antonio, Texas, to watch classic films like *Escape from New York*.

Rodriguez created amateur home movies with a JVC video cassette recorder while he was a boy, but when he enrolled at the University of Texas in 1991, he discovered his dream profession had a costly barrier to entry.

Rodriguez had an idea for an action film about a musician set in Mexico. Lacking the money to realise his vision, he enrolled as a paid subject in a clinical experiment at a drug research facility. He used the USD7,000 pay cheque from these tests to pay for the cost of shooting his debut film *El Mariachi*.

Because he had so little money, Rodriguez embraced constraints as a way of becoming *more* creative.

To reduce expenses, Robert didn't hire a film crew, he took on many of the roles himself, and he encouraged the few actors in the movie to help with behind-the-scenes work. Instead of setting up sound recording equipment, Robert shot in silence and dubbed the audio in post-production.

Rodriguez even froze the action every few seconds and changed the camera angle to give the film the appearance of having multiple cameras. And instead of buying squibs for the shootout scenes, he used condoms filled with fake blood fixed over weightlifting belts.

He completed the film using his USD7,000 pay cheque, and while describing his bare-bones approach to film-making in his book *Rebel Without a Crew*, he tells aspiring filmmakers:

> "The creative person with limitless imagination and no money can make a better film than the talentless mogul with the limitless chequebook every time. Take advantage of your disadvantages, feature the few assets you may have, and work harder at them than anyone else around you. When given an opportunity, deliver excellence and never quit."

Rodriguez originally meant for *El Mariachi* to be released to the Mexican home video market, but film executives at Columbia Pictures were so impressed with his achievements on a budget, that they bought the distribution rights and helped Rodriguez market the movie.

El Mariachi went on to win multiple international awards and spawned two sequels, *Desperado* and *Once Upon a Time in Mexico*. In 2011, *El Mariachi* was selected for preservation in the United States' National Film Registry.

Today Robert Rodriguez is an accomplished director, producer, screenwriter, editor and musician. He is also the man behind film franchise like *Spy Kids* and the *Mexico* trilogy. Even though Rodriguez has more financial and creative freedom today, he goes out of his way to impose artificial constraints around all of his creative projects.

He recently said, "I want all of my movies to not have enough money, to not have enough time, so we are forced to be more creative."

The Freedom of Restrictions

The Irish singer-songwriter Damien Rice is another creative master who sometimes uses a lack of resources to accomplish more.

In 1998, Damien Rice (1973–) was the front-man for the Irish band Juniper. They'd signed a six-album record deal with PolyGram and their two singles, *Weatherman* and *World is Dead,* were a critical and commercial success in Ireland.

So when Damien quit the band to travel across Italy and busk around Europe, Juniper's fans were shocked.

Damien and I went to the secondary school Salesian College in Celbridge Co. Kildare, although he was several years ahead of me. In 2000, I interviewed Damien for the school paper, and I asked him why he quit on success.

Damien explained he disliked creating radio-friendly music.

"And where do you see yourself in ten years?" I asked.

"It's not where I see myself going," he said. "It's who I see myself as."

I was struck by Damien's intense approach to his art.

He still wanted to record music, but he lacked the resources of a band, having other people to rely on and most importantly of all, a major label record deal.

Between 1998 and 2002, Damien wrote and composed all the tracks on what would become *O* on a shoestring budget. His track *Older Chests*, for example, features a sample of cars passing by and the laughter of a group of school children on the street. Damien couldn't afford to hire kids to come into the studio, and he didn't hire a producer to create this sound for him.

Instead, Damien took his microphone and recorder, stood at the gates of a primary school in Celbridge, and recorded the chatter of children as they finished school for the day. The result is something more natural and authentic sounding than a studio recording.

When he released *O* in 2002, it became a success in Ireland, the United Kingdom and the United States thanks to songs like *Volcano* and *the Blower's Daughter.*

Damien did what he did in a pre-smartphone, pre-YouTube world. He used what he lacked (money, the understanding of his peers) to ground his work. Some years later I stumbled across an interview with Damien where he said:

> "A kite needs to be tied down in order to fly. I learned how important restrictions can sometimes be in order to experience freedom."

Today, it's much easier for musicians to create on a shoestring budget and get their music out into the world. You can use restrictions and creative limitations (like lacking a record deal or having the resources of a studio) to lend an authenticity, a freshness and a sense of urgency to your work that isn't possible when you're successful.

Instead of ruminating about what you need, your lack of resources can help you ground a project and learn more about the creative process.

Getting Your Technique Down

New York-man Robert Mapplethorpe (1946-1989) wanted to do one thing with his life: to live for art. During his teens and early twenties, he experimented with drawing, painting and sculpture.

Then, in 1970 a friend gave Robert a loan of a 360 Land camera, a clunky but technically simple, silver and black device. Robert settled on the camera as his creative tool of expression because "it was more honest."

At first, Robert restricted himself to only taking pictures of his former girlfriend and life-long creative partner the singer Patti Smith. The confines of a single muse shaped his creative vision and enabled him to hone his technique. In *Just Kids*, Patti writes:

> "He was comfortable with me and he needed time to get his technique down. The mechanics of the camera were simple, but the options were limited."

That wasn't the only restriction Robert faced. In the 1970s, camera film was expensive, and Robert couldn't afford the liberty of mistakes. So, he made every shot count.

Robert developed his technique and visual eye with the 360 Land Camera and later a Polaroid. In 1973, he held his first solo photography exhibition at the Light Gallery in New York.

With success came more financial and creative resources. A patron bought Robert an expensive Hasselblad camera (a type of camera previously used to photograph the moon landings).

Although a professional-grade camera gave Robert more choices and control over his use of light, he didn't learn anything about the creative process from having access to more powerful tools.

According to Patti, "Robert had already defined his visual vocabulary. The new taught him nothing, just allowed him to get exactly what he was looking for.

Robert wanted to document New York's S&M scene, and his subsequent exhibition shocked audiences, but impressed his peers. He said:

> "I don't like that particular word 'shocking.' I'm looking for the unexpected. I'm looking for things I've never seen before ... I was in a position to take those pictures. I felt an obligation to do them."

Robert went on to photograph a series of male and females nudes, delicate flower still lifes and portraits of artists and celebrities. He also collaborated intensely with the world's first female bodybuilder Lisa Lyon.

He continued to push photography forward as an art form until he died of AIDS in 1989.

Today, Robert is regarded as one of the twentieth century's most provocative visual artists, and his work is displayed in galleries around the United States, South America and Europe.

Working Around the Margins of The Day

In 2013, after several difficult months out of work, I started a full-time job in a profession that I wasn't entirely comfortable with.

Before I started this job, I set out to write my first non-fiction book *A Handbook for the Productive Writer*. As my day job took over, I found I didn't have much time or energy in the evenings to write my book. I wrote less and less each day until finally, my progress ground to a frustrating halt.

I told myself it was okay to push out publishing this book because nobody was breathing down my neck looking for a first draft.

Besides, I'd just started a new job. *I should go easier on myself.*

As the weeks went by, this felt more like an excuse and less like a genuine reason for not writing my book.

Then, I read James Altucher's *Choose Yourself.*

He lays out a bold case for why creative people need to consider themselves as entrepreneurs in charge of their destiny.

Altucher believes if we don't take charge of our creative lives, no one else will. We must choose ourselves. He writes.

> "The key slogan is, "Keep failing until you accidentally no longer fail." That's persistence."

Was I just making excuses? Was I a mediocre entrepreneur? Was I just another failed writer? I looked in the mirror and said, "Yes, yes, and yes."

I knew then something had to change.

I didn't know what to do until I read about *Parkinson's Law*. The British historian and author Cyril Northcote Parkinson put forward the argument in the 1950s that "work expands so as to fill the time available for completion." It's since been applied to many other fields, including the arts.

In other words, even if I had all day to write, it still wouldn't feel like enough time.

So I faced a crucial decision: I could either put off writing my book until I settled into my new job and had some free time. Or I could use my lack of time as a boundary for my work and commit to writing the first draft, even if it meant getting up an hour or two before work and giving up television, computer games and other passive leisure activities in the evening.

I chose the latter and while the first few weeks were hard, writing around the margins of the day forced me to work faster.

Some of my sentences weren't as tight as they could have been and some of my arguments needed fleshing out. But like a runner who stumbles over a pothole in the road and keeps going, I didn't stop to fix each mistake because I didn't have time (at least during the first draft).

Thanks to my self-imposed deadline, I turned around an admittedly rough first draft within a month or two, which I then spent another two months editing and polishing.

When the time came to self-publish the book, I was as busy in work as I ever was and I realised if I'd put off writing the book and hadn't used constraints to finish it, I would have still been in the same place.

I'd like to tell you the book was a critical and commercial success. *It wasn't, but here's the thing:*

When I self-published the book, I didn't care about my lack of obvious success. I discovered I was the kind of person who could take an idea, work it out and finish it; and even if I never sold a copy, I felt like I'd accomplished a small, personal victory.

Over the next few weeks and for the first time in my life I received emails from readers who told me things like:

"I was pleasantly surprised at how Bryan Collins's A Handbook for the Productive Writer lives up to its promise.

As the author of over 40 books and thousands of articles and blog posts, numerous ideas resonated with my experiences...but, even more important, there were numerous hacks and suggestions that were new to me.

Bryan's writing engages you from the start, yet he doesn't waste a word. Topics are concisely covered with admirable detail and momentum. An excellent guide for both new writers and those in need of a quick recharge."

I also received more critical reviews like this:

"This book has a lot of good content especially for the beginning writer. I will definitely put some of his suggestions into action. But... wading through all of the mistakes makes this a difficult read."

I won't lie; the critical reviews were hard to take. After I read this one, I hired another editor to help me fix these mistakes before relaunching the book. Then, I stopped writing it and moved on with my life.

Establishing a boundary around my work helped me write, finish and ship it and teach me more about the act of writing.

While the book isn't perfect, finishing it and getting real-world feedback from readers – *living, breathing readers* – was motivating enough to drive me to start and finish a second (and better) book.

The Power of Constraint

Limitations aren't confining; they're liberating.

Creative masters like Robert Mapplethorpe saw chaos around them and brought order to it. What better way to bring order than to restrict yourself to a few chosen tools, a big idea or means of expression?

If you were told you could write, draw, film or paint anything you liked using any material imaginable, it would be difficult to know where to start.

On the other hand, if you were given a creative brief that required you to write 1,000 words about the importance of storytelling or sketch Dublin city at dawn using charcoal, these restrictions would force your brain to come up with more inspired ideas.

You can overcome creative overwhelm by narrowing your choices.

For example, if you don't have the freedom to work on your ideas for eight hours straight because you have a job or other personal commitments, use the constraint of time to create what's most important to you first thing in the morning or at night.

Don't be afraid of a looming deadline; use it as a catalyst to drive yourself and your project forward.

Or if you lack the financial resources to conclude your project, reduce, remove and simplify your work and then finish what you can afford.

You can always come back to the unfinished parts of your creative project later on. An idea that matters doesn't demand a million dollar budget and five years of development.

Creative masters like Robert Rodriguez, Damien Rice and Robert Mapplethorpe imposed constraints on their works rather than seeking out unlimited resources. These constraints helped them learn more about the creative process.

When you have too much freedom, getting started or finishing your work can feel impossible. On the other hand, artificially imposed constraints will help you come up with better ideas and give you an end goal to work toward.

It will narrow your creative vision and help you focus on what's important.

Creative Takeaways

- Do you lack enough time or money to finish your creative project? Use your lack of resources to narrow the scope of your project.
- Rather than being concerned about what you lack, use what you have to finish your creative project.

6

BECOME AN HONOURABLE THIEF

"Immature poets imitate; mature poets steal; bad poets deface what they take, and good poets make it into something better, or at least something different."
– T.S. Eliot

TWYLA THARP HAS A SECRET WEAPON.

There is nothing particularly mystical, secretive or expensive about her weapon. It's a simple cardboard box from Home Depot, but Twyla has won many creative victories with it.

In the summer of 2000, Twyla (born 1941) invited the artist Billy Joel to her home in Manhattan. There, she showed Billy the first item from her box: a twenty-minute videotape of dancing to his compositions, like *Uptown Girl* and *Big Shot*.

After seeing the video, Billy told Twyla, "I didn't know my stuff could look so good."

Feeling encouraged, Twyla took two blue index cards from the box for Billy to see. On the first index card, she'd written, "Tell a story" and on the second she'd written, "Make dance pay."

Billy wanted to know more, so Twyla pitched her vision for a Broadway musical show called *Movin' Out*. She envisioned composing and choreographing a dance show set to twenty-seven Billy Joel songs.

Twyla's dance show would depict the lives of five kids from Long Island from 1965 to 1984, set to the backdrop of the Vietnam War.

Billy agreed to Twyla's big idea.

As a composer and dancer with over 40 years of experience, Twyla has choreographed dozens of award-winning ballet shows, and she has worked on numerous films and TV shows including *Hair* and *The Golden Section*.

Over the coming months, Twyla added to her cardboard box of ideas.

She included Billy's CDs, the opening line of Homer's *Illiad*, tapes of the singer's live performances, Billy's lectures, television and radio footage from the Vietnam War and movies like *The Deer Hunter* and *Full Metal Jacket*.

She also included books from that period like Michael Herr's *Dispatches* as well notebooks of little ideas, photos of Billy from the 1970s, song lists, and notes Twyla gave to her music director for the show.

The musical *Movin' Out* premiered in 2002. It won two Tony awards and became an international success.

Twyla fills a box with ideas like this for almost every creative project.

On the front of each box, Twyla writes the name of her creative project, and then she fills the boxes with newspaper clippings, CDs, notebooks, pictures, pieces of art, videotapes of her dancing and more. She organises for these shows by gathering ideas from books, films, music, shows and more and then reflecting on what she finds.

Even if Twyla doesn't know what her big idea is about or where she's going, the act of filling a box helps her commit to a big idea. The box inspires Tharp and fuels fresh thinking for her shows. The filling of a box is a creative ritual that protects Twyla from forgetting a good idea or from feeling uninspired.

In *The Creative Habit*, Twyla explains:

> "The box makes me feel connected to a project. It is my soil. I feel this even when I've back-burnered a project: I may have put the box away on a shelf, but I know it's there. The project name on the box in bold black lettering is a constant reminder that I had an idea once and may come back to it very soon."

Tharp is a creative master who knows where to look for ideas, and she looks everywhere. She looks to the wider world, the work of her contemporaries and even to her past success.

Sometimes after a show ends, Tharp takes an old box from storage, and she goes through her old ideas to see what inspired her and to trace the roots of her creative projects. Twyla believes old ideas sometimes suggest new ones:

> "For me, personally, a successful piece is a piece that suggests the next one – that put me in a place where I have the energy and the vision to move forward and tackle a whole other approach to something."

Like Tharp, keep a box and fill it with what inspires you. It doesn't have to be a physical cardboard box either. Use a notebook, a scratchpad, a Dictaphone, a journal, your computer or whatever works. Don't obsess about the box or your research process because to do so is to procrastinate.

The river doesn't care what you bring down to the bank. Your creative tool is less important than having a place where you put ideas from books you read, art you admire, films you watch, museums you visit, music you listen to, from the conversations you share and even from your dreams.

Once these ideas are safe, review what you have and search for common themes, as Tharp did when she went through her cardboard box of ideas and discovered Vietnam as the theme that would unite the characters in her Billy Joel musical.

Once you cultivate a habit of gathering ideas and working through your findings, you'll be able to combine these old ideas in new and exciting ways.

What Steve Jobs Did

Steve Jobs (1955-2011) was a creative master who knew what he wanted, and in 1979 he wanted to see what was inside the Xerox PARC.

A Xerox research centre in Palo Alto had become a place for technologists and top computer scientists like Alan Kay to research big ideas and work without interruption.

At that time, using a computer was a daunting affair. The touch-screens and point and click systems we take for granted today didn't exist. Instead, computer users typed relatively complicated commands into an expensive and far from intuitive computer.

Kay famously said, "The best way to predict the future is to invent it."

Along with his team at Xerox PARC, he wanted to make computers more accessible to the general public and particularly for small children.

To realise their dream, a team at Xerox PARC invented a user-friendly graphical interface for a small personal computer, known as a DynaBook.

In a precursor to today's Windows and OS X operating systems, the screen of their computer had documents and folders on it and users controlled the DynaBook using a point and click device instead of typing cumbersome commands.

While Kay's team worked on their big idea, Xerox's venture capital division was negotiating the details of a one million dollar investment in Apple.

In 1979, Apple was one of Silicon Valley's most attractive new technology companies and a year away from its initial public offering (IPO).

The Apple management team accepted Xerox's investment on the condition that they show Jobs and his engineering team what was going on inside Xerox PARC. At the time, Xerox believed it was getting the better bargain.

They were wrong.

When Jobs and his engineering team saw the graphical interface under development inside Xerox PARC, they couldn't believe how far the technology had advanced. Jobs later told his biographer Walter Isaacson:

> "It was like a veil being lifted from my eyes. I could see what the future of computing was destined to be."

Xerox's three-button mouse cost USD300 to build and the computer itself cost an eye-watering sixteen thousand dollars, a sum beyond the means of the average consumer. Jobs immediately set about creating a similar interface, but they constrained themselves with a tight budget.

In just six months, his Apple engineering team adapted PARC's ideas, improved the graphical interface and rolled-out a number of other cost-saving engineering changes. Jobs's team invented a single-button Apple mouse that cost just USD15. The Apple team also added icons, a menu bar to the graphical interface as well as an ability to open files and folders by double-clicking with their cheaper Apple mouse.

They built on a pre-existing idea from Xerox PARC and they created the Macintosh operating system. Later, Apple released the inexpensive Apple Lisa computer, a machine that the general public could both afford and use. Apple went on to sell millions of Silicon Valley's most famous products.

Years later, Jobs said:

> "If Xerox had known what it had and had taken

advantage of its real opportunities...it could have been as big as I.B.M. plus Microsoft plus Xerox combined – and the largest high-technology company in the world."

Today, computer historians point to the Xerox PARC incident as one of the greatest heists in corporate history, perhaps in part because Jobs famously said:

> "Picasso had a saying–'good artists copy, great artists steal'–and we have always been seamless about stealing great ideas.

Here's the thing: Jobs and his team didn't shamelessly steal a big idea from Xerox PARC and hawk it as their own. Instead, they built on a pre-existing idea that was good but unfinished. Nobody was going to buy a computer that cost sixteen thousand dollars.

Using their business expertise, insight, and knowledge of their customer, Apple solved problems like the DynaBook mouse being too expensive and cumbersome to use. They evolved what the team at Xerox PARC started.

Then, Apple did something the team at Xerox PARC failed to do: they shipped a computer that consumers wanted and could afford.

Don't feel too bad for the team at Xerox PARC. Although Xerox withdrew from the personal computer industry altogether, an engineering team at Xerox PARC led by Gary Starkweather went on to invent the laser printer and earn billions for the company.

Jobs did more than steal other people's ideas. He built a career and a company out of gathering old ideas and transforming them into new ones that solved problems for people. Consider what Jobs did when he took to the stage of the Moscone Centre in San Francisco in 2007.

It was a pre-touchscreen smartphone world. Most consumers controlled their phones with ugly buttons, listened to their favourite music and accessed the Internet on separate, clunky devices.

Dressed in blue jeans, white trainers and a black turtleneck, Jobs

told the world he was going to introduce three revolutionary products: a widescreen iPod with touchscreen controls, a mobile phone
and an internet communications device.

He flicked between iOS icons representing these three old ideas.
Then, Jobs revealed how Apple had combined these ideas the first
version of the iPhone:

> "Are you getting it? These are not three separate
> devices, they are one device and we are calling it
> iPhone!"

Consumers owned mobile phones, Internet communications
devices and portable music players before Jobs's big reveal, but
nobody had brought together these technologies like this.

Like many big ideas, the first iPhone was far from perfect. It
lacked many features that mobile phone users now take for granted
such as Bluetooth for connecting to other devices, 3G for accessing
the Internet and the ability to copy and paste text.

Apple offered consumers a powerful (if unfinished) computing
device that redefined the mobile phone product category.

They eventually added these missing features to their big idea
and transformed the iPhone from a rough and unfinished device into
one of the world's most popular pieces of technology.

The story of the iPhone (and the Apple Lisa before it) demon-
strates how creative masters like Jobs *gather* pre-existing ideas,
combine them and then *transform* these old ideas into something
fresh, into a big idea that people want.

Trace the Path of Your Creative Heroes to Infinity and Beyond

Are you worried about taking other people's ideas? Do you fear this
will get you into trouble or that stealing an idea isn't the work of
creative people? Or perhaps you don't have Steve Jobs's swagger or
Twyla Tharp's years of experience?

Francis Ford Coppola, the filmmaker behind films like the *Godfather* and *Apocalypse Now*, offers you this advice:

> "We want you to take from us. We want you, at first, to steal from us, because you can't steal. You will take what we give you and you will put it in your own voice and that's how you will find your voice. That's how you begin. And then one day someone will steal from you."

The filmmakers at Pixar must have been listening to Francis when they created Buzz Lightyear. He's a determined and brave space-ranger. As one of the heroes of the Pixar film *Toy Story 2*, he will go to great lengths to protect his friend Woody and the other toys. But even the affable Buzz has a nemesis.

Throughout *Toy Story 2*, he is pitted against his nemesis, the evil Emperor Zurg. During the final act, Buzz Lightyear and the rest of the toys face almost certain defeat at the hands of Zurg. There comes a moment when the emperor is about to defeat Buzz in an elevator shaft, and all looks lost for the toys.

Zurg says, "Surrender Buzz Lightyear. I have won."

Buzz replies, "I'll never give in. You killed my father!"

Emperor Zurg says, "No, Buzz. I *am* your father!"

Before Zurg can defeat Buzz, Rex Dinosaur knocks Zurg off the top of the elevator with his tail, and he falls down the elevator shaft.

This scene mirrors the climax of *Star Wars: The Empire Strikes Back*. In this film, a triumphant Darth Vader defeats Luke Skywalker and cuts off his hand in an epic lightsabre battle.

Then Vader says, "Obi-Wan never told you what happened to your father."

Luke replies, "He told me enough! He told me you killed him!"

Vader says, "No, I am your father."

He then asks Luke to join him, but Luke throws himself to his apparent death rather than take Vader's side.

Nobody could accuse the *Toy Story 2* filmmakers of stealing unethically from the writers of *Star Wars*. Instead, this climatic *Toy Story* 2 scene is one of the funniest moments of the Pixar film because if you know anything about contemporary cinema, you'll appreciate the obvious nod to *Star Wars* and marvel at this humorous retelling of a classic story.

Filmmakers regularly reference artists they look up to, quoting famous lines and pointing to well-known scenes in films they admire. Instead of being angry about what filmmakers do, we relish their fresh take on old ideas.

When you do the same, do so with honour. Always hide what you take in plain sight. Tip your hat to the source and provide a way for readers, viewers or listeners of your work to trace the roots of your ideas. Cite your sources if you must.

Standing on the Shoulders of Your Creative Heroes

As an artist, you already have a love for stories, books, films, poetry, art and more, but it's not enough to love art, you must study your chosen medium with the diligence of Twyla Tharp and the intensity of Steve Jobs.

When you find a writer you admire, study the reference section of their books and read the work of authors that influenced them.

When you feel the hand of a filmmaker, a poet, a musician or an artist on your shoulder, look deep into their work until you find what keeps them up at night, until you discover what they put inside their cardboard boxes.

Consider the difficult choices the artists overcame while creating their masterworks. Examine the small details of their ideas, pull at the seams and change what you can. Then, insert your personal stories and ideas into their works.

Copy what these other artists do, at least at first.

Would you have done things differently? Is there a way you can remix what they created with the voice of another creative expert?

Taking apart another person's work and then putting it back together will help you understand the process behind their big ideas and figure out what inspired them.

Francis Ford Coppola told you to do it. Steve Jobs wants you to do it. Twyla Tharp showed you how she did it.

Set time aside to consider art you intensely dislike or feel uncomfortable with too. Reading a bad book, listening to a bad album or watching a bad film occasionally gives you a frame of reference between what works and what doesn't. It will also help you find where your boundaries lie so you can later cross them.

Later on, like Jobs, you can improve or combine old ideas or like the Pixar team, you can retell these ideas in new ways.

If you spend time trying to come up with an original idea alone, you won't get very far.

Instead, point to established ideas and explain what they mean to you. Be for or against them, apply them, retell them and transform them.

When you use your voice or tell your story, these old ideas become something else entirely.

They become yours.

Creative Takeaways

- Don't have a box or a file of ideas yet? Write down a list of what inspired you today.
- Pick one writer, artist or creative person that you admire. Trace their influences as far back as you can go.

7

CULTIVATE INTENSE CURIOSITY

"The desire to know is natural to good men."
– Leonardo da Vinci

WHEN WAS the last time your ideas got you into trouble?

I love asking difficult questions, but I've learnt hard lessons from other peoples' answers.

Several years ago, I was employed as a care worker in a large service for people with intellectual disabilities. I supported ten men and women in living independent lives in two different houses in a suburb an hour outside of Dublin, Ireland.

Much of my job involved performing regular household maintenance and hygiene checks around two large bungalows.

I ensured the toilets were clean and that there was enough to eat in the fridge. I balanced the houses' financial accounts, paid bills on behalf of the service users and brought them shopping for food.

It was my job to do all of the things necessary to keep the two houses running just as I would with my own. The only caveat was that I documented a significant part of what I did every day in various report books, and I also administered medication.

I enjoyed spending time in the company of the service users, but I hated almost everything else about my job. I sometimes had to work overnight shifts for 12-24 hours and sleep in a small, cramped bed next to the office desk and afterwards, I had little energy for anything worthwhile.

I felt as if the unwavering routine, the tedious hygiene checks, and the stifling policies were turning me into an anxious, depressed and prematurely bald man in his early thirties.

One day, my manager called me into the office for a personal review. These discussions took place every three months, and they served as a means for managers to assess the performance of their team.

I sat on the bed next to the desk.

My manager pulled a large grey folder from the small wooden shelf, slapped it on the table and adjusted her black narrow-frame glasses.

"I'd like you to re-read this Bryan." She pushed the grey folder towards me.

I picked up the folder and edged away from her.

The hygiene policy was a heavy grey document. It contained pages and pages about the various household chores we had to complete each day including vacuuming, dusting, cleaning the toilets and so on. It also went into great detail about the tick-charts we had to complete.

I put the policy back on the office desk. "If I spend all day doing these cleaning exercises, how will I have time to take the service users out for coffee or to meet their friends?"

(A big part of the social care profession involves teaching people the independent living skills many of us take for granted.)

"Find time Bryan," she said. "Why is it when you're on shift, the house is never clean enough? You have to make sure there are no crumbs in this toaster. I need you to dust behind the back of the presses. We're getting this place ready for a big hygiene inspection, and you're letting the place down."

"Why do we have to do this?" I tried not to look at the tuft of blonde hair on her lip. "Will this feel like a normal home for the men and women who live here if we're going around inspecting the toaster every morning? I don't even engage in this madness in my own house. How will any of *this* teach these men and women the skills they need to succeed in the community?"

My manager held her head and said,

"Just for once Bryan, I wish you would stop asking me questions. I didn't make this up. It's the service policy, it's your job, and you need to do it."

"Why should we follow policy blindly?"

"If you have a problem, Bryan why don't you take it up with HR?"

I mumbled something about doing better and walked out of the office.

At the time, I thought I was a model employee because I was speaking up, but I can see now how I complicated life for my manager. She was doing her best to comply with regulations and policies that she had no control over.

Although the work we were doing in the community was important and satisfying (I enjoyed being able to help the men and women live full and independent lives in the community), I couldn't handle the day-to-day rules and regulations.

It's in my DNA to ask questions and wonder why I should do things one way and not another. It's in my DNA because, after school, I trained for four years as a journalist.

In university, our lecturers rammed home the importance of speaking up to authority, of considering why authority says 'this is how we do it', of asking difficult questions.

This interrogative questioning translates to the realm of investigative journalism, but it'll get you in trouble in areas of life. Nobody likes asking or answering difficult questions whether they be about themselves, their work or their ideas.

However, if you want to tap into your inner genius and become more creative, intense curiosity is a skill you must cultivate. You need to establish whether your big idea is one you should act on or set down because your time and resources are limited.

This is an approach creative masters take.

Why Leonardo da Vinci Wants You to Cultivate Intense Curiosity

The creative master Leonardo da Vinci (1452-1519) was an engineer, chef, writer, artist, inventor, humourist, musician, painter, architect, political advisor, designer, botanist, civil planner and more.

His most famous paintings include the *Mona Lisa*, *The Last Supper* and *Virgin on the Rocks*, his most famous sculptures include *da Vinci's Horse in Bronze*, and his most famous inventions and drawings include the helicopter and the parachute.

So how did Leonardo da Vinci achieve so much in 70 years?

While he was a genius, da Vinci cultivated intense curiosity about everyone he met and everything he came across. He asked difficult questions and used the answers to inform his inventions, ideas and creations.

Da Vinci kept dozens of notebooks and journals throughout his life, many of which still exist. In these, he recorded how he spent days roaming the countryside searching for answers to things he didn't understand.

He wanted to know why shells existed on top of mountains, why lightning is visible immediately, but the sound of thunder takes longer to travel, how a bird sustains itself up in the air and so much more.

Da Vinci wandered the streets of Florence and often bought caged birds from the Italian merchants, opened the cages and watched the birds fly into the sky so he could understand these creatures.

He studied and drew flowers and plants from multiple angles to better understand their anatomy. According to the scholar Michael Gelb, da Vinci wrote in a journal:

> "Do you not see how many and how varied are the actions which are performed by men alone? Do you not see how many different kinds of animals there are, and also of trees and plants and flowers? What variety of hilly and level places, of spring, rivers, cities, public and private buildings; of instruments fitted for man's use; of diverse costumes, ornaments and arts?"

Da Vinci didn't confine his intense curiosity to botany and nature either. He interrogated his paintings by placing them against a mirror so he could better judge their strengths and weaknesses. He even dissected human bodies to understand how our bags of flesh and bones work. He wrote about his intense curiosity:

> "These questions and other strange phenomena engage my thought throughout my life."

Da Vinci's approach is exhausting, and I'm not advocating dissecting human bodies. However, you can develop a da Vincian type of intense curiosity, interrogate your big ideas and figure out which ones to act on and which ones to discard by asking one simple question repeatedly:

Why?

The Five Whys

Taiichi Ohno (1912-1990) had a mission. As a production engineer, he wanted to eliminate waste and inefficiency for the production processes he was responsible for at Toyota.

As a shop floor supervisor, Ohno knew firsthand how many components Toyota stockpiled for its production line at great expense. When he became an executive, he adopted a da Vincian approach to this problem and asked senior management why the company adhered to such a costly solution.

Not satisfied with their answers, Ohno kept asking "*Why?*" until he got to the root of why the company believed it needed its stockpiles.

Ohno also questioned why Toyota needed to buy specialised, expensive and difficult to customise machines when general purpose, smaller machines were cheaper, could produce a wider variety of parts and be reconfigured.

He developed his method of interrogative questioning into a problem-solving tool known as the Five Whys. He then set out instructing engineers at Toyota how they could use the Five Whys to fix and prevent issues every day on the manufacturing line.

When confronted with a problem, have you ever stopped and asked why five times? It's hard to do even though it sounds easy. Ohno used the example of a machine that stopped functioning:

1. **Why did the machine stop?** There was an overload, and the fuse blew.
2. **Why was there an overload?** The bearing was not sufficiently lubricated.
3. **Why was it not lubricated sufficiently?** The lubrication pump was not pumping sufficiently.
4. **Why was it not pumping sufficiently?** The shaft of the pump was worn and rattling.
5. **Why was the shaft worn out?** There was no strainer attached, and metal scrap got in.

Repeating "why" five times like this can help uncover most problems and address the underlying causes.

If this procedure were not carried through, one might simply replace the fuse or the pump shaft. In that case, the problem would occur again within a few months.

The Toyota production system has been rebuilt on the practice and evolution of this scientific approach. By asking and answering "why" five times we can get to the real reason for the problem, which is often hidden behind more obvious symptoms.

The Five Whys became a problem-solving tool at Toyota and

other manufacturing companies. In the same way, you can solve creative problems and figure out what to do next by applying it to your work.

Several years ago, I kept a blog called WorkReadPlay. Over the course of a year, I published posts about productivity, technology, games and other ramblings.

As my website traffic grew, I discovered many visitors left after they landed on my site. I couldn't figure out how to convince people to read my work.

I knew I needed help, so I joined a blogging training programme, and I asked a mentor to review my website. He told me the name of my site was confusing visitors.

The term 'WorkReadPlay' didn't communicate what my blog was about, and my website visitors had little patience for figuring it out for themselves. I wasn't happy with his analysis because changing a site name is a lot of work. So, I used the Five Whys to figure out what to do next:

1. **Why do I want to rename my blog?** The current name is confusing for new visitors, and they leave almost immediately.
2. **Why is this name confusing?** The terms Work, Read, and Play don't relate to the articles that I write about, and I often find myself having to explain to people what this word means.
3. **Why doesn't this name relate to the articles I write?** I'm more interested in publishing articles about writing and creativity than I am in posting articles about work, books, games or life in general.
4. **Why am I more interested in writing these types of articles?** I feel more confident writing these kinds of articles, it's what I'm passionate about, and this sort of writing will enable me to become a better writer and even help people.

5. **Why do I want to become a better writer and help people?** So I can earn a living from my writing and find more meaning from my work.

It took me ten minutes to ask the Five Whys. In the same way, this creative problem-solving tool will help you overcome creative challenges and identify the cause of what's holding you back.

Now that you understand how to ask better questions about your big idea, you'll need a place to record your answer.

The Creative Power of Journal Writing

Whether you like to write or not, journalling is an ideal practice for thinking through your big idea. It will help you identify negative thought patterns, set goals and track your progress, and articulate your arguments and ideas privately.

You can also reflect on recent lessons from your personal or professional life and mark your accomplishments and failures.

I've kept journals in various forms for ten years. It's entertaining and sometimes worrying to read back on personal and professional journal entries from several years ago.

A journal isn't about impressing others with your ability to craft a great sentence. Instead, it serves as a place for you to ask better questions and record your answers. These could include:

- What do I know about my big idea?
- What do I need to find out about my big idea?
- What's wrong with my big idea?
- What's inspired about my big idea?
- Why do I want to create this?
- Why do I feel blocked?
- Why does this inspire me?
- How can I approach my big idea in an original way?

- What will happen if my big idea fails?
- What will happen if my big idea succeeds?

Some people want to keep a journal but say that they find the process time-consuming, that they forget to write regular entries and that they don't know what to write.

If you're experiencing these problems, accept that there will be times when you don't or can't write. You don't have to write long or literary entries. Sometimes one-hundred or even two-hundred words will be enough to consider your idea in a new way.

Yes, journal writing demands commitment, consistency, and honesty, but the creative process will impose these on you anyway.

Start Asking Better Questions Today

I was a care worker in the community for two difficult years.

Finally, after a spending a weekend ticking charts, cleaning toasters, dusting behind the presses, administering medication, teaching service users how to shop and cook for themselves, checking the household car for defects and writing lengthy reports about everything I did or didn't do, I came home and argued with my wife.

"I can't deal with the depth of madness in that place, and my manager is complaining about my inability to clean the place," I said. "They want us to be caretakers, cleaners, doctors, nurses, mechanics personal assistant and more, and it's never enough. Why do I have to put up with their unrealistic expectations?"

"You don't," my wife said.

"What do you mean?"

"If you hate the job so much, why don't you just quit?"

"That's a ridiculous idea," I said. "I need a paying job. Why would you say something like that? You don't understand what I've to put up with."

"I understand more than you realise."

I went upstairs to write about our argument, but instead I re-read old entries from my journal. I paused when I found this one:

"After I had come home from work last Thursday, I sat in the car outside the house for twenty minutes in silence. When I managed to go inside, I could barely speak to my wife. It was all I could do to go straight to bed.

Last night I had a review. [My manager] said she wished I was less argumentative. She told me I need to make more of an effort with the house cleaning.

She has a point, but what galls me is being criticised for not cleaning the crumbs out of a toaster. Crumbs in a fucking toaster? Maybe we should all live in cellophane wraps and never leave our disinfected and whitewashed beds?

This morning, HR told me they're not calling me for an interview for a promotion because the director of nursing doesn't recognise my qualification.

Is this the shove out the door I need rather than the hand on the shoulder that says, "Stay a while longer?" Why am I wasting my time in a job I hate?"

If I knew about the Five Whys several years ago, I would have quit my job immediately, but even being forced to answer one 'why' was enough for me to reconsider my wife's suggestion.

Over the course of a few weeks, I realised I was working somewhere that didn't value creativity or curiosity from its employees.

I handed in my notice.

It took another two years (and a stint of unemployment) before I found satisfying work, but I wouldn't change how things worked out.

Asking why got me into trouble, but it also helped me figure out I was the wrong person in the wrong job.

Curiosity can be a dangerous thing.

Most people don't like asking difficult questions because they're afraid of the answers. They might have to quit a job they hate, abandon a big idea they love or pivot the direction of their creative project in a more challenging direction.

You and I know better.

We anticipate unexpected problems. We recognise them as signs we're asking the right questions. We understand that cultivating intense curiosity is the best way to figure where we're going with our big idea and what we should create next.

Creative Takeaways

- Got a creative problem? Ask 'why' five times until you get to the root of it.
- Start a journal about your creative project and record your progress each day. Write like no one will read it.

8

BE OPEN, BE PURPOSEFUL

"While you're being creative, nothing is wrong, there is no such thing as a mistake – any dribble may lead to the breakthrough."
– John Cleese

WE TAKE this substance for granted today, but in the 1830s, the western world was in the grip of rubber fever. A series of inventors were determined to earn money from selling waterproof fabrics, clothing, tubes and storage implements all made from rubber.

They faced a number of problems.

Natural rubber is messy and inelastic. It freezes solid during cold winters and turns into a glue-like substance during hot summers. Within five years, many of the companies selling natural rubber goods went bankrupt, and people agreed natural rubber had no future.

A self-taught chemist from Connecticut by the name of Charles Goodyear (1800–1860) took exception to common wisdom about rubber. Goodyear dedicated his life to his one big idea: that he could treat natural rubber and transform it into a usable substance for the mass-market.

"There is probably no other inert substance which so excites the mind," he said about rubber.

Goodyear experimented unsuccessfully with the material for years throughout great personal hardship and often on the verge of bankruptcy.

Six of his twelve children died in infancy, and he was imprisoned for being unable to pay his bills. His regular exposure to dangerous chemicals like nitric acid, which he used to treat rubber, harmed his health, and he even almost accidentally suffocated himself.

Goodyear hit a turning point in 1839. He went into the Woburn general hardware store in Massachusetts to sell a sample of natural rubber combined with sulphur and white lead to prospective buyers.

While showing his product to a sceptical audience, Goodyear accidentally threw a fistful of gum onto a hot potbellied stove. It sizzled and turned hard under the heat, and when Goodyear scraped the substance off the stove, he found the rubber charred like leather.

Most men would have seen this as an embarrassing disaster but not Goodyear. He realised that heat held the key to treating natural rubber.

An almost bankrupt Goodyear spent the following winter figuring out how much heat he had to apply to natural rubber and for how long to achieve this effect. Eventually, he discovered that applying steam to rubber under pressure for four to six hours provided the required results.

Goodyear denied his discovery of vulcanization was a mere happy accident.

Instead, he insisted the hot stove incident held meaning only for someone "whose mind was prepared to draw an inference," for someone who had "applied himself most perseveringly to the subject."

If you want your mind to draw an inference between different ideas, like Goodyear, you must open yourself up to what's possible.

And if you want to apply yourself perseveringly to your subject, be purposeful about how you act on your big ideas.

Open Yourself Up

Goodyear probably didn't feel at ease pitching his wares in a hardware store full of sceptics, and there's no need to put yourself through this additional torment; it's hard enough to unlock fresh thinking.

To open yourself up to better ideas like Goodyear, you'll need time, space and freedom to think, which is why the early mornings or late at night are ideal for creative projects.

Once you're there, relax your focus. It helps to read a book or listen to music you love before you start and then to prepare your workspace for making a mess.

You should feel more relaxed, playful, and even humorous about your work and about making mistakes.

Cultivate an environment where there are no consequences, bad ideas or expectations to perform. For thirty or sixty minutes let it be enough to have fun with your crazy ideas, to embrace the chaos. Embrace curiosity for its own sake and see where it takes you.

When you do, absurd ideas will float to the top of your mind, and you'll find it easier to grab them and draw elaborate connections between different concepts.

Having fun is an essential element. If something doesn't feel like work, you're more likely to enjoy what you're doing or at least think differently about the challenges you're facing. If a creative project feels like work, inspired thinking is less likely.

Opening yourself up means experimenting, playing with the ridiculous and asking questions like:

- What would happen if...?
- Wouldn't it be even better if...?
- Let's pretend
- Go on

John Cleese is a British actor and comedy writer famous for films like *A Fish Called Wanda* and the *Monty Python* series, as well as television shows like *Fawlty Towers*. An expert on creativity, he describes opening your mind up to new ideas as being in the open mode.

He says:

> "The open mode is a relaxed, expansive, less purposeful mode in which we are probably more contemplative, more inclined to humour... and consequently more."

Cleese, like many creative masters, plays with his problems when he wants to open himself up to new ways of thinking. He avoids coming to a decision about what needs to be done and finds time for exploration and happy accidents by creating as free an atmosphere as possible for himself and those he works with. He says:

> "It's a mode in which curiosity for its own sake can operate because we're not under pressure to get a specific thing done quickly. We can play and that is what allows our natural creativity to surface."

Like Cleese, try new forms of creative expression that you haven't mastered and see where they go. To find new ideas that matter, allow yourself to commit mistakes and only later decide which of these you want to fix and which ones belong in the bin.

At first, you may not have a clue as to what a great idea looks like or what you'll do when one arrives. Although Cleese likens being open to having fun, it also takes guts to do something new.

Zoom into a single detail in your work (as Goodyear did with his sizzled piece of rubber), play around with your arrangements and see if your ideas unravel or tighten up.

Then zoom out, take the wider view and explore what would happen if you changed the medium, the form or the direction of your idea.

Once you've unlocked new ideas or found a way of thinking differently about your work, it's time to put what you've come up with into action.

Be Purposeful

If being open helps you become a more creative artist, being purposeful will help you become a more productive artist.

To be purposeful is to adopt an active state of mind wherein you focus entirely on the task at hand.

Being purposeful is what you do when you're under deadline, when you face multiple demands or when you're at work.

This mindset feels exciting and sometimes anxious. There's pressure to achieve a goal within a certain timeframe, and that pressure spurs you into concentrated action.

It's what Charles Goodyear did after the incident in the Woburn general hardware store when he set out to determine how much heat to apply to treat natural rubber. Goodyear knew what he needed to do; he just had to figure out how to accomplish this goal.

John Cleese likens being purposeful to being in the closed mode. He says:

> "We have inside of a feeling that's there's lots to be done and we have to get on with it if we're going to get through it all. It's an active, probably slightly anxious mode, although the anxiety can be exciting and pleasurable.
>
> "It's a mode in which we are probably a little impatient if only with ourselves. It has a little tension in it, not much humour. It's a mode in which we are very purposeful and it's a mode in which we can get very stressed and even a little bit manic but not creative."

Be purposeful when you need to accomplish a series of set tasks under a tight deadline. To integrate this thinking into your creative work, eliminate as many distractions as possible from your studio. Turn off email, the television or even distracting background music.

And so on.

Your routine and the work before you is all that matters. Don't stop to ask 'Why' or ponder your motivations. If for example, you're about to jump out of a plane, it's unhelpful to consider the myriad of absurd uses for a broken parachute. Focus on nailing your landing.

Remember, you're on the hook for meeting a deadline, for finishing a project on time and for realising the demands of others.

Ask yourself what's the next action for your creative project.

If you are creating as part of a team, ensure everyone knows what they are doing, and they have what they need to finish on time.

Do everything in your power to complete this action and push your creative project towards its inevitable and final outcome.

But what should you do if the scale of your project is overwhelming?

If that's the case, then chunk or break down your creative work into smaller, more digestible pieces. Tackle each of these pieces in the most efficient way possible using your limited resources.

Let's say I want to research a scene for a short story that's set in a Spanish seafood restaurant.

First, I'll write down everything I have to research about this scene on a list. This may include finding a picture of the restaurant, figuring out the food on the menu, determining the location of the restaurant and writing down descriptions of the restaurant's employees and clientele.

Next, I allocate a 15-minute period during which I research these items and nothing else. Later on, I'll concentrate on writing the scene in question. When it's time to write this scene, I avoid feeling overwhelmed about what I need to do because I have everything I need in one place, and I don't have to alternate between researching and writing.

Similarly, as a writer with a blog I sometimes write down a list of everything I need to do when I log into my website. This list may include: uploading images, revising old posts and preparing the following week's post. I try to do these activities one after the other when I log in.

By listing out these steps, I don't waste time repeatedly logging into my site to perform these tasks during the week. I can spend more time writing and less time tinkering with my blog and others things that will pull my attention from my work.

Chunking your tasks will help you get more from the hours in your day and avoid wasting time wondering what you need to do and when.

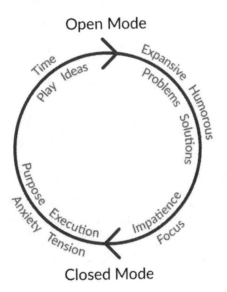

Lowering the Drawbridge

When I've a series of set tasks to perform or a To Do list to tick off, I dive in. I relish knowing what to do and when, the march towards a deadline, a completed project or published article.

Now don't get me wrong, I'm not superhuman.

Like Cleese says, when I face too many demands, I feel anxious about a project failing or letting someone down.

So, I pause what I'm doing, and I remember, if I have the energy and the persistence to complete the dozens of daily tasks that form my day or if I have the guts to go back and renegotiate my deadlines, I'll get there.

I don't pause for long because when you're purposeful, there's little room for self-doubt. I don't have hours to waste wrestling my fears: that I'm not good enough, that what I'm doing will bring shame to my friends and family, that I'm inventing shit as I go along.

Onward.

I'm more comfortable with being purposeful than I am with opening myself up because when I lower the drawbridge, I invite loneliness inside.

Cleese talks about the humour of being open, but I've found it to be a darker place than the one he describes.

I get up early, and I sit at my desk, and I type. There, sandwiched between the hours of six and eight am, I look at the clock, and I wonder "How much longer?" and "Can I really do this?"

I lack clarity about what I need to do. I often can't see the solution to whatever creative problem I'm working on. There's no immediate feedback about the quality of my ideas and whole days go by where I produce nothing of value. I have to remind myself production isn't the point.

I have time and space, and it'll have to be enough because turning up is a part of life.

When you're purposeful, the worst that can happen is you will let others down. When you open yourself up and lower the drawbridge, you risk inviting inside loneliness, boredom and self-doubt. Although these may be unwelcome guests, you must trust they come carrying gifts.

What do I mean by gifts? Well, if you look closely at your uncomfortable emotions, vulnerabilities, inner fears and desires, you'll find new ideas that you can use for your creative work.

Can you use the times your parents told you weren't good enough and that you'd end up in prison one day?

Can you bring the awful sense of isolation we'll do anything to escape from and turn it into a bold and original work?

Can you expose how we complain about being too busy to get anything done when we're just putting off our most important work?

Can you use the loneliness, guilt and sense of disconnect that comes with spending so much time alone with your ideas?

Can you use the time you lay in bed awake at three am, your daughter sick with the flu, worrying about being fired and your hair turning grey?

Can you describe the party where you drank half a bottle of absinthe, insulted the host and passed out in the bathroom?

Can you tell us about shouting at your six-year-old son to hurry up for school, him trudging behind you unhappily to the child-minder and then later that day coming home from work to find he'd tidied the back garden. He wants to know, 'Are you happy with me now, Dad?'

And so on.

Ok, I've ripped some of these examples straight from the negative thought processes that keep me up at night but please don't get me wrong.

I share them here (not because I want to) but to show you that being open isn't always fun, and that you must do it anyway. The world doesn't respond to homogeneous fluffy pink clouds. Even John Cleese once wrote an angry little stand-up comedy routine based on his painful and expensive second divorce.

And what did he call the tour?

Alimony.

Great ideas speak a universal truth, at the core of which are real and often painful experiences like divorce and emotions like anger. And of course, when you open up your veins onto the blank page or the virgin canvas, there's no guarantee that anyone will like what you leave behind. That's the risk you have to take.

People will judge you, and they could even dislike you, and that's less attractive than being the type of person who gets things done, but it's real creative work.

Your Reward

Now naturally, creativity isn't a tidy process whereby you calmly walk from A to B to C and get to the end of your project without encountering problems along the way. No matter how much you prepare and plan, understand that to write, to perform, to compose is messy.

Being open to new ideas and being purposeful about how you act on them doesn't guarantee you financial or professional success either.

Today, treated rubber is one of the most commonly used substances in the world. It's in your car, your clothes and even your computer and global demand for the substance will be worth USD158 billion by 2018. Considering the value of rubber, you'd think Goodyear died a wealthy man. You'd be wrong.

Even after discovering the correct formula for the vulcanization of rubber, Goodyear struggled personally and professionally.

The British inventor Thomas Hancock patented the vulcanization process in the UK eight weeks before Goodyear, and Goodyear also had to fight a series of legal cases in the States against people who stole his ideas.

He died in 1860 some USD200,000 in debt, but despite his apparent lack of success, did he die a bitter man?

No. Goodyear cared less about the outputs from his creative work and more about the effort he'd put into growing his big idea. A master of his inner genius, for Goodyear, it was enough to go to the river with his bucket and draw from it over and over.

He wrote, "Life should not be estimated exclusively by the standard of dollars and cents. I am not disposed to complain that I have planted and others have gathered the fruits. A man has cause for regret only when he sows and no one reaps."

Creative Takeaways

- Spend fifteen minutes playing with your creative project this week. Take a responsible, creative risk.
- If you're struggling to finish one of your ideas, break it into chunks that you tackle day-by-day.

9

UNLOCKING YOUR INNER GENIUS

CREATIVE HEROES LIKE HENRI MATISSE, Steve Jobs and Twyla Tharp can teach us how to accomplish our dreams and overcome setbacks. Look to their lives and their work when your own is faltering, and you need new ways of overcoming troubling creative impasses.

My first creative hero was the English author Roald Dahl (1916-1990).

I came across him when I was five while reading books like *The BFG* and *James and the Giant Peach*.

He was the first author who showed me what's possible with the written word.

Dahl wasn't always a writer. As a young man, he worked for Shell in Kenya and Tanzania and spent his free time hunting. During World War II, Dahl became a decorated fighter ace and intelligence officer.

He shot down at least two enemy Ju-88 planes, took part in the Battle Of Athens and was one of the last pilots to withdraw from Greece during the German invasion.

When he started to write, Dahl wasn't afraid to draw from the river of his old life for his new creative one. He wrote several short stories about his time as a fighter pilot and drew extensively on his previous careers in his novels and short stories.

In James and the Giant Peach, the seagulls (or fighter aeroplanes) attack the giant airborne peach, a talking centipede falls (or parachutes) off the giant peach, and the end of the book references air raids and heroes returning home (from the war).

Then, in *Going Solo*, Dahl writes:

> "I was already beginning to realise that the only way to conduct oneself in a situation where bombs rained down and bullets whizzed past, was to accept the dangers and all the consequences as calmly as possible. Fretting and sweating about it all was not going to help."

Dahl was a disciplined creative professional too. He came down to the river with his bucket, writing for two hours each morning and evening in a 6ft x 7ft shed at the back of his orchard in Buckinghamshire, in the United Kingdom.

In his shed or "little nest," Dahl kept a comfortable chair, a lamp, a system for storing his files, a wooden desk and various writing utensils.

Each day after he wrote, Dahl ate a bar of chocolate and crunched the wrappers up into a ball. He also covered the walls with pictures of his family, ideas for stories and other personal mementos.

I like this story about Dahl best of all:

Like many creative people, Dahl was having trouble finding a good idea for a project he was working on. One day while sitting behind dozens of moving cars, he suddenly thought of a breakthrough for his story.

Dahl looked around the car for a pen or a pencil to write down his idea, but he couldn't find anything and he grew afraid he'd forget his idea before getting home.

(If you ever had the unsettling experience of coming up with a great idea in the shower, while cooking, driving, walking or doing something else, you'll understand Dahl's fear.)

Now, Dahl wasn't the type of creative person to let a good idea flow through his hand.

So, he opened his door, and with his finger, he wrote the word 'chocolate' into the dirt on his car. This small little act of plunging his bucket into the river was enough for Dahl to remember his idea, and it became *Charlie and the Chocolate Factory*.

He later said about his ideas, "You work it out and play around with it. You doodle... you make notes... it grows, it grows..."

Your Bucket Is Overflowing

Ideas are exciting. If you plunge your bucket deep enough into the river, you'll have more than you know what to do with.

Quench your thirst with the teachings, works and thoughts of creative masters you admire. Drink deeply from the buckets of their powerful big ideas, the crazy little ideas and even those other ideas people missed.

Ask how you can apply their approaches to your work. Intense curiosity is why creative masters like Leonardo da Vinci and Steve Jobs were successful in multiple fields like art, engineering and business. They took what worked in one field and applied it to the next.

Now, I talk about Steve Jobs, Twyla Tharp and Roald Dahl, but there's just one problem with heroes. Their achievements are so lofty that it can hurt to wander through Dream Country for too long.

When this happens to you, put down your hero's work and look to your environment. A walk through a field, a farmer cutting hay, a snippet of music, a snapshot from your dream could spark fresh thinking if you let it.

Start creating something of your own, make messy mistakes, move past them and keep at your craft.

Practice opening your mind to the wider world because to be an outsider is to possess a perspective creative masters crave.

From the moment you held a guitar, a pen or a paintbrush in your hands, you may have known what type of creative person you are, but if you haven't had this startling experience, don't worry.

Taking little risks and experimenting with form, and substance will teach you more about a craft than any moment of inspiration, introspection or deep study ever can.

So, keep turning up in front of the blank page or the canvas.

Don't feel like any of this is a waste of time. Setbacks and dead-ends are par for the course.

Eventually, something will pop out onto the page, the screen or your sketchpad and you'll wonder: *"Where did that come from?"*

As you develop your creative practice, you'll be able to transfer your skills from one project or medium to the next and solve problems faster. You'll know what to borrow, what to use and what to pour back into the river.

You are your own golden ticket.

AFTERWORD

If you enjoyed this book, please rate this book and leave a short review. Reviews like yours help me write more books like this one.

Finally, if you have feedback about this book you always email bryan@becomeawritertoday.com. I'd love to hear from you.

WAIT!

DID YOU CLAIM YOUR FREE BONUS?

VISIT
BECOMEAWRITERTODAY/POCBONUS.COM

ABOUT THE AUTHOR

In this life, Bryan Collins is an author.

In another life, he worked as a journalist and a radio producer. Before that, he plucked chickens. He is passionate about helping people accomplish more with their writing projects and when he's not writing, he's running.

Bryan makes his online home at www.becomeawritertoday.com. There, he writes about writing, creativity and productivity. His work has appeared on *Fast Company*, *Lifehacker* and *Copyblogger*.

Bryan holds a degree in communications and journalism, a diploma in social care, a masters degree in disability studies and a diploma in digital media.

You can reach him on Twitter @BryanJCollins, email bryan@becomeawritertoday.com or join his Facebook page Become a Writer Today.

Bryan is also the author of *A Handbook for the Productive Writer: 33 Ways You Can Finish What You Started* as well as the novella *Poor Brother, Rich Brother*.

He lives an hour outside of Dublin.

www.becomeawritertoday.com
bryan@becomeawritertoday.com

TOOLS FOR BECOMING MORE CREATIVE

Below is a list of tools I use and rely on as a writer and blogger. I've also included some other recommended resources that will help you with your creative work.

The list is relatively long and (depending on the nature of your creative work) you won't need to use all of these tools.

Remember, the creative process and your ideas are more important than any tool.

99designs

In the past, I've used 99Designs to find a designer to create a book cover for one of my books. If you want a professional design (like a logo, a t-shirt, business card or packaging) for your online business, 99Designs is a good place to start.

A smartphone

The best camera is the one you have with you at the time and if you need to take a picture (or just capture an idea), your smartphone is almost always the best choice. I use an iPhone.

A whiteboard

I keep a large whiteboard next to where I write. It's a great way of capturing and organising ideas. I also use it for mind maps and for creating outlines for articles, chapters and even books. I also find a whiteboard less confining that traditional digital tools.

Audible

As a creative person, your inputs (what you read, listen to and watch) are just as important as your outputs (what you write, paint or draw). I spend at least an hour a day listening to audiobooks on my smartphone that I purchased from Audible. If you sign up, they'll give you your first audiobook for free.

Behance

A showcase site for design and other creative work. It's great for inspiration and also for finding designers to work with. Also, see Dribble.

Brain.FM

Brain.FM provides AI-generated music for focus, relaxation and deep work. When I use this, I find I can enter a state of creative flow faster. Plug in a pair of headphones and you're good to go.

Buffer

I use Buffer to share articles, photos and social media updates by myself and others on Instagram, Facebook, LinkedIn, Twitter and Pinterest. Buffer simplifies sharing social media updates across multiple networks and enables you to schedule your updates in advance.

You can also collaborate with others and enable them to manage your social media profiles... leaving you more time to work on your creative projects. More advanced social media users should consider Meet Edgar.

Canva

For years, I used Photoshop and the rest of the Adobe Suite to create images. Today, I rely on Canva because it simplifies creating images using a drag-and-drop editor.

Creative Commons

This site will help you legally share your work online and find a license or copyright that suits your business model, website or project.

The site's search tool will also help you find images, music and other media that you can use in your creative projects, commercial or otherwise.

Dragon Dictate

I use Dragon Dictate to dictate early drafts of blog posts, book chapters and articles. This piece of software enables me to write faster, and it also reduces the amount of time I spend struggling with RSI. In this article, I explain how to get started with dictation.

Evernote

If I have an idea that I don't want to forget, I keep it in here. I also save articles I like into Evernote as part of my personal swipe file. Sometimes, I take photos of mind maps on my whiteboard with my phone and put them in Evernote too. It's my digital brain.

Image sites

Gratisography contains awesome and free high-resolution photos that you can use for your creative projects, as does All The Free Stock and Death to Stock.

I recommend Depositphotos for premium stock images. Alternatively, you could take the images yourself and apply an Instagram filter. Designers can get icons on the Noun Project.

Freedom

If you keep getting distracted while writing, use the app Freedom. It will disable your internet access for a pre-determined period, allowing you to focus on writing and not on cat videos!

Grammarly

If you need help proofing your work, I always recommend you hire a proofreader. However, I also recommend Grammarly as another line of defence and for checking your writing as you go.

Google Docs

I use Google Docs to write on the go and to track my progress in spreadsheets. I also collaborate with other writers and creative professionals, and *it's free*.

G Suite (formerly Google Apps for Work)

It's time to put the hard-drives and USB keys away. Essentially, G Suite enables me to send and receive emails from the 'Become-AWriterToday.com' domain (bryan[at]BecomeAWriterToday.com) using the Gmail interface.

I also get lots of additional cloud storage and can easily collaborate with other writers, editors and designers. This isn't free, but it's affordable.

Headline Analyzer

This free online tool will check your headlines and give you practical tips for improving them so they are more emotional and captivating. Alternatively, consider CoSchedule Headline Analyzer.

Headspace

This is my meditation app of choice. If you've never meditated before, Andy Puddicombe will teach you the basics through guided lessons. Alternatively, check out these free guided meditations by Tara Brach.

Hemingway App

If you're not a confident writer, don't worry. This app will review your text and, in the spirit of Ernest Hemingway, it will tell you what to remove or edit so your writing is bold and clear.

Kindle Spy

KindleSpy is a great tool that will help you see which books are selling on Amazon and how much they earn. Then, you can use this information to increase sales of your book.

LeadPages

I use LeadPages to create landing and squeeze pages for my books. I also use it to create sign-up forms for my mailing list.

Your bed or chair of choice

Fact: napping is conducive to creativity. Just ask Salvador Dali. The trick is to wake yourself up after twenty minutes so you avoid going into a deep sleep. Then, when you wake, get straight to work.

Noise cancelling headphones and an album of instrumental music

A good set of noise cancelling headphones will help you concentrate on your work no matter where you are. Each morning, I don my pair and listen to albums like *Rain for Sleeping and Relaxation* on repeat while I write.

(Yes, that album is exactly like the name sounds.)

iMindMap/MindNode/MindMeister

I've used these affordable tools to create mind maps in the past. They're easy to learn too. Alternatively, you can create a mind map using pen and paper.

Medium

Do you just want to write and share your ideas online, but you're not interested in running a blog? Medium removes all of the technical challenges of blogging and helps you connect with readers.

New Rainmaker

I use this tool for hosting and managing my website. It comes with some powerful tools for writers and bloggers, and it includes security, backups and other essential blogging services for one monthly price. Alternatively, consider Siteground.

Oblique Strategies

In 1975, the producer and musician Brian Eno and the artist and painter Peter Schmidt created a deck of cards that give musicians and artists constraints within which to work.

These constraints foster the kind of lateral thinking creativity demands. Essentially, you draw a card at random from the deck and are presented with a prompt like: 'Do the words need changing?'

You can buy the deck or use a free, web-version.

Pilot G4 Pen and a Moleskine notebook

No, there's no need to use a Moleskine notebook for writing or capturing ideas, but I'm drawn to the build quality of these note-books and the feel of the paper. I've a box full of these near where I write.

Even if you're not drawn to these admittedly expensive notebooks, working on your ideas with a pen (you can't go wrong with the Pilot G4) and paper will liberate fresh thinking.

Screenflow for Mac

This is a great tool for recording video and screencasts. It's also relatively simple to edit your recordings and export them to a format suitable for Facebook, YouTube or your website. Alternatively, consider Camtasia.

Scrivener

I can't recommend Scrivener enough. I use it to write blog posts and books. I've used Scrivener to write feature articles for newspapers, reports, ebooks, a thesis and even a novel.

>> Get my free blogging template.

Other useful writing apps include Ulysses, Pages and IA Writer.

SumoMe

SumoMe is an all-in-one tool that enables you to gather email addresses, set up a share bar on the side of blog posts and also track how people interact with your work online. If you're sharing your work online, this is highly recommended.

Upwork

No matter how talented or hard-working you are, it's impossible to do everything alone. UpWork is a great service for finding designers, editors and more who can help you with time-consuming tasks so you can spend more time on your book, art or music.

I've used Upwork to hire video-editors and also developers who fixed problems on my website.

ACKNOWLEDGMENTS

Thanks to Command+Z Content for their great editing and Martine Ellis for proof-reading. Thanks to Terri Black for the book cover design. And finally, thanks to you for reading.

GET THE POWER OF CREATIVITY SERIES

Book 1: Learning How to Build Lasting Habits, Face Your Fears and Change Your Life

Book 2: An Uncommon Guide to Mastering Your Inner Genius and Finding New Ideas That Matter

Book 3: How to Conquer Procrastination, Finish Your Work and Find Success

Www.thepowerofcreativitybook.com

REFERENCES

Books

Altucher, James. *Choose Yourself,* James Altucher, 2013.

Bales, David and Orland, Ted. *Art and Fear.* Image Continuum Press, 2001.

Campbell Joseph and Moyers, Bill. *The Power of Myth*, Anchor Books, 1998.

Catmull, Ed. *Creativity Inc: Overcoming The Unforeseen Forces That Stand in the Way of True Inspiration.* Random House, 2014.

Csikzentmihalyi, Mihaly. *Flow: The Psychology of Happiness.* Ebury Publishing, 2002.

Covey, Stephen R. *The 7 Habits of Highly Effective People.* Free Press 1989.

Dali, Salvador. *50 Secrets of Magic Craftsmanship.* Dover Publications, 1992.

De Bono, Edward. *How to Have a Beautiful Mind.* Ebury Press, 2008.

Duhigg, Charles. *The Power of Habit: Why We Do What We Do In Life and Business.* Random House, 2012.

Eric Reis. *The Lean Startup: How Today's Entrepreneurs Use Contin-*

uous Innovation to Create Radically Successful Businesses. Crown Business, 2011.

Gelb, Michael. *How To Think Like Leonardo da Vinci: Seven Steps to Boosting Your Everyday Genius.* Harper Collins, 2009.

Gladwell, Malcolm. *Outliers: The Story of Success.* Back Bay Books, 2011.

Godin, Seth. *Tribes.* Hachette Digital. 2008.

Godin, Seth. *All Marketers Are Liars.* Portfolio. 2012.

Green, Robert. *Mastery.* Viking, 2012.

Gregoire, Carolyn and Kaufmann, Scott Barry. *Wired to Create: Unraveling the Mysteries of the Creative Mind.* TarcherPerigee, 2015.

Harris, Sam. *Waking Up: A Guide to Spirituality Without Religion.* Simon & Schuster, 2014.

Isaacson, Walter. *Einstein: His Life and Universe.* Simon & Schuster, 2008.

Isaacson, Walter. *Steve Jobs: The Exclusive Biography.* Machete Digital, 2011.

Kahneman, Daniel. *Thinking, Fast and Slow.* Farrer, Straus and Giroux, 2011.

King, Stephen. *On Writing Well: A Memoir of the Craft.* Hodder and Stoughton, 2010.

Kleon, Austin. *Show Your Work.* Workman Publishing Company, 2014.

Kleon, Austin. *Steal Like an Artist.* Workman Publishing Company, 2012.

Levy, Mark. *Accidental Genius: Using Writing to Generate Your Best Ideas, Insight and Content* (Second Edition). Berrett-Koehler Publishers, 2009.

Newport, Cal. *Deep Work: Rules for Focus in a Distracted World.* Piatkus, 2016.

Rodriguez, Robert. *Rebel Without a Crew.* Plume, 1995.

Segal, Zoe Gillian. *Getting There.* Harry N. Abrams, 2015.

Tharp, Twyla. *The Creative Habit: Learn It and Use It For Life.* Simon & Schuster, 2014.

T.S. Eliot. *The Sacred Wood: Essays on Poetry and Criticism*. <u>Bartleby.com</u>, 2009.

Waitzkin, Josh. *The Art of Learning: An Inner Journey to Optimal Performance*. Free Press, 2007.

Wilboue, Edwin Charles. *Victor Hugo By A Witness Of His Life*. 2007. Accessed at <u>https://archive.org/stream/victorhugobyawit003274mbp/victorhugobyawit003274mbp_djvu.txt</u> *on* March 15, 2016

Audio, Videos and Films

The American Reader. *This Day In Lettres: 3 April (1855): Charles Dickens to Maria Winter*. Accessed at http://theamericanreader.com/3-april-1855-charles-dickens-to-maria-winter/ on May 22, 2016.

Cleese, John. *Lecture On Creativity for Video Arts*. 1991. Accessed at <u>https://www.youtube.com/watch?v=Qbyoed4aVpo</u> on November 22, 2015.

Ferris, Tim. *The "Wizard" of Hollywood, Robert Rodriguez*. Four Hour Work Week, 2015. Accessed at The Tim Ferris Experiment <u>http://fourhourworkweek.com/2015/08/23/the-wizard-of-hollywood-robert-rodriguez/</u> on November 22, 2015.

Greenberg, Robert. *Great Masters: Mozart-His Life and Music*. The Great Courses, 2013.

Pink, Daniel. *The puzzle of Motivation*. 2009. Accessed at TED <u>http://www.ted.com/talks/dan_pink_on_motivation/transcript?language=en</u> on November 22, 2015.

Lasseter, John et al. *Toy Story*. Pixar Studios, 1995.

Lasseter, John et. al. *Toy Story 2*. Pixar Studios, 2000.

Lucas, George et al. *Star Wars: A New Hope*. Lucasfilm, 1977..

Kershner, Irvin et al. *Star Wars: The Empire Strikes Back*. Lucasfilm, 1980.

Jobs, Steve. *iPhone 2007 Presentation (Full HD)*. Accused at <u>https://www.youtube.com/watch?v=vN4U5FqrOdQ</u> on December 4, 2015.

Articles, Research Papers and Essays

Altmann, E. M. & Trafton, J. G. *Task interruption: Resumption lag and the role of cues. Department of Psychology*. Michigan State University, 2004.

Asimov, Isaac. *How Do People Get New Ideas? MIT Technology review,* 2014. Accessed at https://www.technologyreview.com/s/531911/isaac-asimov-asks-how-do-people-get-new-ideas/ on April 17, 2016.

Baird, Benjamin et. al. *Inspired by Distraction: Mind Wandering Facilitates Creative Incubation.* Psychological Science, 2011. *Accessed at http://pss.sagepub.com/content/early/2012/08/31/0956797612446024.abstract* on May 9, 2016.

Brogan, Jan. *When being distracted is a good thing.* The Boston Globe, 2012. Accessed at https://www.bostonglobe.com/lifestyle/health-wellness/2012/02/27/when-being-distracted-good-thing/1AYWPlDplqluMEPrWHe5sL/story.html on May 22, 2016.

Coyle, Danie. *A Gauge for Measuring Effective Practice.* The Talent Code. Daniel, Coyle, 2009. Accessed at http://thetalentcode.com/2011/05/31/a-gauge-for-measuring-effective-practice/ on May 9, 2016. .

Clear, James. *The Akrasia Effect: Why We Don't Follow Through on What We Set Out to Do (And What to Do About It).* 2016. Accessed at http://jamesclear.com/akrasia on March 15, 2016.

Dumas D, Dunbar KN The Creative Stereotype Effect. PLoS ONE 11(2): e0142567. doi:10.1371/journal.pone.0142567. PLOS, 2016. Accessed at http://journals.plos.org/plosone/article?id=10.1371/journal.pone.0142567 on May 22, 2016.

Ericsson, Anders K et al. *The Role of Deliberate Practice in Acquisition of Expert Performance.* American Psychology Association, 1993.

Howie, Hugh. *My advice to aspiring authors.* The Way Finder, 2013. Accessed at http://www.hughhowey.com/my-advice-to-aspiring-authors/ on June 24, 2016.

Kageyama, Noa. *The Most Valuable Lesson I Learned from Playing the Violin.* The Creativity Post, 2012. Accessed at http://www.creativitypost.com/arts/the_most_valuable_lesson_i_learned_from_playing_the_violin on May 22, 2016.

Kelly, Kevin. 1,000 True Fans. The Technium, 2008. Accessed at http://kk.org/thetechnium/1000-true-fans/ on June 24, 2016.

Herbert, Wray. *Ink on Paper: Some Notes on Note Taking.* Association for Psychological Science, 2014. Accessed at http://www.psychologi-calscience.org/index.php/news/were-only-human/ink-on-paper-some-notes-on-note-taking.html on May 22, 2016.

Mac Kinnon, Donald. *The Identification of Creativity.* Applied Psychology, 1963.

Mueller, Pam and Oppenheimer, Daniel. T*he Pen Is Mightier Than the Keyboard: Advantages of Longhand Over Laptop Note Taking.* Accessed at https://sites.udel.edu/victorp/files/2010/11/Psychological-Science-2014-Mueller-0956797614524581-1u0h0yu.pdf on May 22, 2016. Association for Psychological Science, 2014.

Oakley, Keith and Djikic, *Maja. How Reading Transforms Us. New York Times, 2014.* Accessed at *http://www.nytimes.com/2014/12/21/opin-ion/sunday/how-writing-transforms-us.html?_r=0* on September 15, 2015.

Reader's Digest. *The Charles Goodyear Story.* Good Year, 1957. Accessed at *Good Year Corporate.* Accessed at *https://corporate.goodyear.-com/en-US/about/history/charles-goodyear-story.html* on November 22, 2015.

Reis, Eric. *How DropBox Started As A Minimal Viable Product.* 2011. Accessed at http://techcrunch.com/2011/10/19/dropbox-minimal-viable-product/ on April 17, 2016.

Schwartz and Porath. *Why You Hate Work.* The New York Times, 2014. Accessed at http://www.nytimes.com/2014/06/01/opinion/sun-day/why-you-hate-work.html on February 22, 2016.

Sternberg, Jacques. *In Act 2, the TV Hit Man Becomes a Pitch Man.* The New York Times, 2007. Accessed at http://www.nytimes.-com/2007/07/18/arts/television/18madm.html?_r=0 on May 22, 2016.

Walker, Tim. *The Telegraph. Ernest Hemingway never wrote drunk, says granddaughter Mariel Hemingway.* The Telegraph, 2013. Accessed at http://www.telegraph.co.uk/cul-ture/books/booknews/10236200/Ernest-Hemingway-never-wrote-drunk-says-granddaughter-Mariel-Hemingway.html on September 15, 2015.

Wilson, Timothy D et al. *Just think: The challenges of the disengaged mind.* Science Mag, 2014.

Vaynerchuk, Gary. 3 Ways You Need To Be Marketing Your Book

in 2015. Gary Vaynerchuk, 2016. Accessed at https://www.garyvaynerchuk.com/3-ways-you-need-to-be-marketing-your-book-in-2015/ on June 24, 2016.

Ying, Jon. Meet the Team! (Part 1). Dropbox, 2009. Accessed at https://blogs.dropbox.com/dropbox/2009/02/meet-the-team-part-1/ on June 24, 2016.

Made in the USA
Columbia, SC
16 November 2017